Developing a Center for Teaching Excellence

Developing a Center for Teaching Excellence

A Higher Education Case Study Using the Integrated Readiness Matrix

Lawrence A. Tomei, James A. Bernauer, and Anthony Moretti

ROWMAN & LITTLEFIELD
Lanham • Boulder • New York • London

Published by Rowman & Littlefield
A wholly owned subsidiary of The Rowman & Littlefield Publishing Group, Inc.
4501 Forbes Boulevard, Suite 200, Lanham, Maryland 20706
www.rowman.com

Unit A, Whitacre Mews, 26-34 Stannary Street, London SE11 4AB

Copyright © 2016 by Rowman & Littlefield

All rights reserved. No part of this book may be reproduced in any form or by any electronic or mechanical means, including information storage and retrieval systems, without written permission from the publisher, except by a reviewer who may quote passages in a review.

British Library Cataloguing in Publication Information Available

Library of Congress Cataloging-in-Publication Data
ISBN 978-1-4758-2611-1 (cloth : alk. paper)
ISBN 978-1-4758-2612-8 (pbk. : alk. paper)
ISBN 978-1-4758-2613-5 (electronic)

∞™ The paper used in this publication meets the minimum requirements of American National Standard for Information Sciences—Permanence of Paper for Printed Library Materials, ANSI/NISO Z39.48-1992.

Printed in the United States of America

Contents

Preface vii

Acknowledgments xi

Introduction xiii

PART I: THE PEDAGOGIES OF HIGHER EDUCATION 1

1 Pedagogies of Teaching and Learning in Higher Education 3

2 Pedagogies of Technology in Higher Education 13

PART II: THE CULTURAL INFLUENCES OF ORGANIZATIONS 23

3 The Culture of Organizations 25

4 The Culture of Higher Education 35

PART III: THE FOUNDATIONAL CONCEPTS OF THE IRM 49

5 Forming the Dimensions of the Integrated Readiness Matrix 51

6 The Skills and Competencies of the Integrated Readiness Matrix 59

7 Determining Your Location on the Integrated Readiness Matrix 67

PART IV: DEVELOPING/IMPROVING A CENTER FOR TEACHING EXCELLENCE 83

8 Building a Center for Teaching Excellence 85

9 Faculty Portfolios for Teaching Excellence 97

10 Invitation to Join the IRM-Network 105

Appendix A: Dominant School of Educational Psychology 111

Appendix B: Action Verbs for the Cognitive Domain 113

Appendix C: Action Verbs for the Technology Domain 115

Appendix D: Recommended Teaching Episodes for IRM Quadrants 119

Appendix E: Building Your Own Teaching Episodes Template 135

Appendix F: Integrated Readiness Matrix Survey Instrument 137

Appendix G: Robert Morris University's Student Engagement Transcript Categories 143

Appendix H: CITADEL Workshops 145

Appendix I: Strategic Plan (Key Elements) 147

Preface

Developing a Center for Teaching Excellence is a follow-up to our first book, *Integrating Pedagogy and Technology: Improving Teaching and Learning in Higher Education* (Bernauer & Tomei, 2015). In the original text, the Integrated Readiness Matrix (IRM) was introduced as a model to facilitate ongoing professional development of higher education faculty. Whereas the first book provided a theoretical roadmap to support faculty development, this book is intended as a practical guide for launching (or improving) a university or college Center for Teaching Excellence. Faculty aspire to improve their instructional practice; the concepts and ideas related to the IRM will foster professional development and guide the development of an institution's Center for Teaching Excellence.

This book is the product of continuous action research and practical implementation. Regarding the validation of the IRM, there has not been widespread use of the instrument thus far and therefore we cannot claim from a quantitative viewpoint that there is an established high degree of concurrent or predictive validity. However, validity itself is a concept that, while initially developed as part of the quantitative tradition, may have limited applicability to our primary concern of providing faculty with a tool that they find useful for finding their own pathway and approach for becoming a better teacher and scholar.

In his article on validity in qualitative research, Wolcott (1990) concludes that "we have labored too long under the burden of this concept" (p. 148) but rather offered suggestions that get to the heart of conducting research that cannot be quantified (pp. 127–135) and that we think is more relevant for the purpose of developing a useful instrument to help faculty incrementally and systematically improve their instructional expertise. However, we will continue to evaluate and improve the IRM as additional evidence is accumulated.

It has been most gratifying that we have been able to collaborate with a doctoral candidate in nursing whose dissertation includes the evaluation and validation of the IRM.

The IRM recognizes the need to facilitate faculty professional development efforts to improve pedagogical and technological expertise. The IRM instrument described in chapter 5 was designed to provide a relatively simple way for individual faculty members to *locate* themselves on a grid that reflects their honest assessment of their current status in relation to pedagogical and technological skills. A high value is placed on both confidentiality and privacy throughout this process since most of us tend to avoid parading any perceived shortcomings in front of public audiences!

In addition, experience and the literature support the notion that faculty are intrinsically motivated to become better scholars and teachers (Marty, 2012). Any changes suggested by college or university administration, including efforts to facilitate professional development, are more widely accepted when such efforts are built upon recognition of this central role of intrinsic motivation.

When initially validating the IRM instrument, it was found that faculty self-perceptions of their technological and pedagogical expertise generally coincided with their placement on the IRM (Bernauer & Tomei, 2015). However, there were also cases where faculty perceptions did not match their location on the IRM after they completed the required steps. In addition, in many cases, faculty were content with their position on the matrix. Their professional development across pedagogy and technology had stalled – some for many years.

It should be noted that faculty were asked to first place themselves in the appropriate quadrant of the IRM based on their own perceptions after reviewing their course objectives and syllabi as well as their own personal assessment, and then were asked to complete the IRM instrument in order to discover the degree of similarity and dissimilarity. Validity was viewed as a match between what faculty believe about themselves as revealed by an inspection of their syllabi compared to their responses on the IRM instrument; some may find this methodology problematic.

However, as alluded to earlier, a fundamental belief is that teaching and learning are first and foremost individual and personal journeys for growing and improving. In the meantime, the exploration of other more *objective* measures of teaching excellence, including outcomes assessment based on student achievement, is under way. The IRM remains an effective tool for helping faculty become better teachers, and such growth in pedagogical and technological skills will ultimately be reflected in a similar growth in the achievement of student learning.

Notwithstanding the IRM instrument as an effective tool for assisting individual faculty members in their efforts to become better teachers, a supportive organizational capacity is key to promoting, sustaining, and rewarding individual efforts. Later in the book, a change in focus will address how education leaders can develop a capacity at their own institutions.

This book should not be considered a final report but rather as a work in progress. As such, we invite our readers to join us in a network to utilize and further refine the IRM and the processes and organizational capacities that support its most effective uses (see chapter 10). We are convinced that growth in expertise in teaching and scholarship is an ongoing process – a moving target so to speak. Rather than see this as a limitation, we see it as an exciting opportunity to engage in continuous learning – isn't that what universities are all about?

REFERENCES

Bernauer, James A. & Tomei, Lawrence A. (2015). *Integrating Pedagogy and Technology: Improving Teaching and Learning in Higher Education*, Rowman & Littlefield Education Publishers, Inc. ISBN: 978-1475809275.

Marty, Thomas (2012). *Are professors in higher education institutions mostly intrinsically or extrinsically motivated to perform research and teaching?* University of Zurich. URL: https://www.researchgate.net/post/Are_professors_in_higher_education_institutions_mostly_intrinsically_or_extrinsically_motivated_to_perform_research_and_teaching.

Tomei, Lawrence (2005). *Taxonomy for the Technology Domain: A Classification of Educational Objectives for the Technology Domain*, Idea Group Publishers, Inc. ISBN: 1591405246.

Acknowledgements

We would like to acknowledge the pivotal role that the faculty at Robert Morris University played in helping us to develop and field test the Integrated Readiness Matrix ((RM). We would also like to acknowledge the support given by our Provost, David Jamison as well as former president, Greg Dell'Omo. We also thank in advance those colleagues from other institutions who will participate in furthering the development of the IRM and its implementation in their respective Centers for Teaching Excellence.

Introduction

The chapters in this book are based on the purpose of serving as a practical guide to help colleges and universities develop the organizational capacity to support faculty in their roles as teachers and scholars. However, even with such a practical focus, it is necessary to include some theoretical basis as context to more fully understand how the Integrated Readiness Matrix (IRM) can be used in Centers for Teaching Excellence to promote ongoing opportunities for faculty development. Chapters 1–4 provide the personal and social context for the case study methodology presented in chapter 8.

Chapter 1: The Pedagogies of Teaching and Learning in Higher Education. In Part 1 of the book, chapters 1 and 2 begin with a description of major learning theories because effective pedagogy needs to be built on the recognition that both we and our students learn in different ways. Learning theories presented are categorized by five major schools, namely: behavioral, cognitive, humanism, constructivism, and connectivism. Because teaching/learning is so complex, there is often a combination of learning theories operating in the classroom. However, each faculty has a perspective that is dominant, consciously or unconsciously, with a propensity to utilize that dominant style in the classroom. So why not build on it?

Chapter 1 offers an exercise that will help determine personal predispositions regarding learning and teaching. Just as importantly, this chapter explains Bloom's Taxonomy that forms the Y-axis of the IRM. The IRM model utilizes this taxonomy to help locate yourself on the IRM matrix in terms of pedagogical skills. Both the metacognitive understanding of preferred learning theories and Bloom's Taxonomy provide the necessary foundation for the remainder of the book.

Chapter 2: The Pedagogies of Technology in Higher Education. Chapter 2 focuses on the technological domain, which comprises the X-axis of the IRM.

Tomei (2005) developed a taxonomy for the technology domain used in this book to understand the levels of technological skills and assist readers in determining their own particular level of accomplishment in this domain. Technology is treated in a unique and somewhat separate fashion from pedagogy. Together, the IRM integrates both good pedagogy and appropriate technology into the higher education classroom.

Chapter 3: The Culture of Organizations. Part 2 begins with chapter 3 and builds on the recognition that organizations play a large role in reaching beyond our own individual capacities. It briefly describes the culture of organizations and the reciprocal influences that are exerted by this culture and the individuals that populate it. Important components of this chapter include organizational development and resistance to change. The chapter provides an understanding of the sociological and cultural influences of organizations as well as the individual characteristics, including the way we view teaching and learning.

Chapter 4: The Culture of Higher Education. Chapter 4 focuses specifically on higher education. Colleges and universities are their own type of organization. Although much of the discussions in chapter 3 apply here as well, higher education has distinct differences. Colleges are engaged in learning and scholarly inquiry less tangible than their more traditional counterparts. Its organizational components are more *loosely coupled*; academic freedom is a fundamental value. Implementation of a system of ongoing professional development via a Center for Teaching Excellence requires an approach that is rooted in both sensitivity toward and a respect for these unique features.

Chapter 5: Forming the Dimensions of the Integrated Readiness Matrix. Part 3 begins the *technical* part of the book, where the IRM and its five quadrants are explained. The chapter presents the essential components of each quadrant and builds a solid understanding of the matrix for subsequent chapters.

Chapter 6: Skills and Competencies of the Integrated Readiness Matrix. Chapter 6 drills more deeply into the levels that comprise the pedagogical and technological axes of the IRM. Bloom's Taxonomy is described in more detail as the pedagogical Y-axis is uncovered. The Taxonomy for the Technology Domain exposes greater details of the technological X-axis. Understanding the actual elements that comprise these taxonomies will expand the basis for ongoing faculty professional development using the IRM. Nearly 70 skills and competencies offered in chapter 6 form the content of a comprehensive faculty professional program.

In addition, the chapter offers a case study template to document your own new workshops, seminars, roundtable discussions, practicum, training sessions, and short courses developed to advance faculty through the quadrants of the IRM.

Chapter 7: Determining Your Location on the Integrated Readiness Matrix. Chapter 7 introduces the mechanics of using the IRM matrix and self-assessment instrument to plot a position on the matrix. It establishes a starting point for recognizing the pedagogical and technological skills already mastered and any shortcomings in faculty preparation in a lifelong journey from apprentice to journeyman to master integrator.

Chapter 8: Building a Center of Teaching Excellence. Practical examples and real-world experiences are effective tools for creating or improving a center of teaching excellence. Part 4 offers a case study of development efforts, implementation practices, and lesson learned for Robert Morris University's Center for Innovative Teaching and Directed Engaged Learning. We call it the CITADEL.

Chapter 9: Faculty Portfolios for Teaching Excellence. In higher education, promotion and tenure decisions are typically predicated on documentation prepared by candidates. This chapter offers a portfolio of teaching excellence grounded in the IRM-containing skill and competency artifacts presented as evidence of professional development by the institution's center of excellence. Portfolios offer evidence of faculty growth: a repository for the collection, working, and showcasing of artifacts that signal participation and mastery of lifelong learning. Reflecting the five quadrants of the IRM, portfolios document personal development from apprentice to master integrator.

Chapter 10: Invitation to Join the IRM-Network. A personal learning network provides an online forum for sharing ideas even if your institution has not yet opened its own center for teaching excellence. Membership is free and gives faculty the opportunity to expand their professional development by networking with higher education experts worldwide. This chapter offers a free community membership to continue a journey into the world of higher education teaching; research to help expand your pedagogical and technological knowledge base to deliver the optimal education experience; and access to educational and professional development opportunities.

This book is a practical guide to help faculty and administrators in higher education to develop a Center for Teaching Excellence that incorporates the IRM as a primary development tool. We welcome your comments using the *IRM-Network* and hope that you join us in our efforts to further develop and refine the IRM approach to develop and mature a center of teaching excellence at your institution.

Part I

THE PEDAGOGIES OF HIGHER EDUCATION

Chapters 1 and 2 not only reintroduce the underlying concepts of Integrated Readiness Matrix (IRM) as described in our earlier book, but lay the foundation for the remaining chapters. Modern effective student-centered pedagogy recognizes that faculty must first appreciate that there are multiple approaches that our students use to learn and these approaches are essentially captured by five *schools of learning* that we describe in chapter 1. Chapter 1 also reintroduces the pedagogical *Y- axis* of the IRM based on *Bloom's Taxonomy* that we argue captures the essential components of the five learning theories. While chapter 1 relies on Bloom's Taxonomy to explain the Y-axis of the IRM, chapter 2 relies on *Tomei's Taxonomy* to explain the role of technology (X-axis). Although we think that technology will eventually be recognized as simply another component of pedagogy, we treat it separately since it still seems perceived as such by most faculty. Based on this assumption, chapter 2 has been designed to help readers see more clearly how technology can be used to improve instructional effectiveness – in fact how it can be integrated into teaching using the IRM as a diagnostic tool. While we encourage readers to read the previous book, we have designed Part One to be a viable substitute for what we describe in our previous book. It is by understanding how students learn that we can develop creative and effective instructional strategies, including its integration with technology.

Chapter 1

Pedagogies of Teaching and Learning in Higher Education

1.1. INTRODUCTION

Learning theories provide faculty with a repertoire of instructional strategies and techniques for facilitating learning. College faculty – especially new college faculty – must come to understand their dominant school of educational psychology. This chapter provides readers with an in-depth probe into personal learning and teaching styles.

How can you teach others if you do not know how you learn? The text begins by introducing faculty to the five most widely accepted schools of educational psychology. The theories of learning, which they represent, offer a foundation for planning, developing, implementing, and assessing instructional activities. Each school interprets the learning process and its implications for the design and delivery of instruction differently.

1.2. SCHOOLS OF EDUCATIONAL PSYCHOLOGY

Faculty must come to understand their own predispositions toward learning in order to appreciate how their teaching choices affect students. They must strive to overcome the inclination to teach in the same way as they learn so that all students in their classroom can experience positive learning outcomes. To provide this grounding, we explore the five schools of educational psychology recognized in the literature, spanning behaviorism of the 1950s and moving forward to current-day connectivism. But first ...

Are you a behaviorist, cognitivist, humanist, constructivist, or connectivist? Let's find out. Appendix A helps to identify primary learning styles. For this exercise to be meaningful, you must regard the school that holds the highest number of *agree* (and fewest *disagree*) responses as your preferred learning style. Also, respond to each statement as a *learner* and not a teacher. Many college faculty regard themselves as *eclectic* teachers, choosing whichever strategy is best for students at the time. While that may work later in your development as a teacher, for now, *identify the most dominant* learning style since most of us tend to teach the way we learn.

1.2.1. The Behaviorist Classroom

For the behaviorist, students' lessons are highly structured, adhering to a strictly sequenced class schedule. A properly constructed learning outcome contains a condition, an action verb, and a criterion that is readily observable and measurable.. Grades are the ultimate learning outcome; do well on the multiple-choice, true–false exams and receive a better grade. All students are categorized in a similar vein; the same standards apply to everyone in the class.

At first glance, college teachers might be tempted to dismiss behaviorism as an unsophisticated teaching modality, appropriate only for the youngest of grade school students. That would be a mistake.

When considering the many ways in which behaviorism can play out in higher education teaching, learning, and management, it is very much alive in the classroom today. For higher education faculty, mastery of behavioral tools remains a suitable strategy – especially for those fundamental, skill-building, core courses that lay the foundation for an academic discipline and, later, a professional career.

If you agreed with the *Statements 1–3* in Appendix A, you are most likely a behaviorist. If so, consider using the following behavioral tools.

- Programmed Instruction. This offers a self-paced instructional package that presents a topic in a carefully planned sequence, asking the learner to respond to questions or statements by filling in the blanks, selecting from a series of alternatives, or solving a problem. Immediate feedback occurs after each response, and students work at their own pace; moreover, the program can be incorporated into books, computers, or personal devices. Classroom learning is presented in small steps so that all students can succeed – one of the fundamental precepts of behaviorist teaching.
- Computer/Technology-Assisted Instruction (C/TAI). This uses the features and strengths of programmed instruction combined with technology to present information in new and different ways. Drill and practice software provides repetition and feedback for designated learning objectives.

Simulation programs imitate real-world experiences and high-level skills that are often impossible, impractical, expensive, dangerous, or too time consuming. Tutorials teach or reteach content materials adapting instruction to student performance.

- Mastery Learning. This emphasizes a student's grasp of specific learning objectives and uses a combination of corrective/remedial instructional alternatives (many technology based) to achieve that goal. Mastery learning assumes that virtually all students can learn what is taught in school if the instruction is approached systematically, help is provided when they have difficulty, sufficient time is slated to achieve the standards established, and there is some clear criterion of what constitutes mastery in the first place. If mastery learning is successfully imparted, almost all students should attain a high score in the examinations.
- Immediate Mastery Quizzes. This is administered in the last few minutes of the class period. When used properly, research shows that learners retain almost twice as much lesson material, both factual and conceptual (Rosenburg, 2013; Smith & Karpicke, 2014; Karpicke & Aue, 2015; and, Weinstein, Nunes, and Karpicke (in press). Administer the quiz to all students, allowing 4–5 minutes per quiz. Share the correct answers and have students grade other group member's quizzes. Continue the process until virtually all students have evidenced mastery.
- Guided Lectures. These are designed to resolve note-taking problems experienced by many underclassmen. A common problem is the undeveloped listening and thinking skills necessary to capture the important content of a lecture. Students are encouraged to listen to 15–20 minutes of lecture without taking notes. Following the lecture, they are given 5 minutes to recall, record, and share their journals with their fellow classmates to reveal any shortcomings in their note-taking and comprehension skills.

1.2.2. The Cognitivist Classroom

The cognitivist believes in ages and stages, convinced that learning is a process that advances from concrete to abstract thinking as learners mature physically and mentally. Effective instruction taps into learners' prior knowledge and expands their *building blocks* of knowledge formed over years of adaptation. Learners either accommodate information as new knowledge or assimilate information into existing knowledge. The cognitivist understands that the thought processes employed to solve problems are every bit as important as the right answer.

If you agree with *Statements 4–7*, you are a cognitive learner who relies on the most tried and tested tools, including the following.

- Discovery Learning. This focuses on active, hands-on learning opportunities for students. At the college level, three main attributes of discovery learning must be considered. First, discovery learning is most appropriate for exploring and problem-solving. Second, any classroom observer would notice evidence of student-driven, consequential, real-world activities in which learners are actively engaged in the process of creating and exploring new knowledge. Third, discovery learning encourages the integration of new knowledge into learners' existing knowledge base.
- Advanced Organizers. They serve three functions and direct the learner's attention to the important material to be presented. They underscore relationships among new concepts. They remind the learner of previous encounters with similar information. If provided by a competent instructor, the college learner uses this tool to quickly organize new material and assimilate (or accommodate) the latest information.
- Active Learning. For the cognitivist faculty, active learning is a prerequisite for learning (especially for adults), and meaningful learning is predicated on cognitively engaged students (Sockalingam, 2012; Brookfield, 1986; Knowles, Swanson, & Holton, 2005). Faculty should convey high expectations from the first day of class; link new knowledge to prior knowledge; provide continuous assessment and feedback; use a variety of teaching modalities; and structure learning in rigorous, active, and accountable ways.
- Determining Students' Prior Knowledge. Some ways that cognitive instructors gage students' prior knowledge include minute papers, performance-based assessments, self-assessments, classroom assessments, and concept maps.

The majority of higher education faculty are advocates of the cognitive school of educational psychology. However, most college faculty are not trained in the concepts and principles of cognitivism that make this modality of teaching a success.

1.2.3. The Humanist Classroom

From the perspective of the humanist, the college classroom is challenging and free from intimidation. Students have a role to play in their own learning outcomes. For college students, choice is built into the curricula of most majors beginning with core education courses offered by the institution and extending into most majors allowing some number of elective courses. Humanist learning involves structuring classes around small groups. While there are a number of best practices for the humanist, cooperative learning offers its clearest implementation for our consideration.

Statements 8-12 describe the humanistic teacher. Here are some tools available for the higher education classroom instructor:

- Cooperative learning. Cooperative learning has been proven to be effective for all types of students, from academically gifted to mainstream students and, for our purposes, college students (Slavin, 1995; Slavin, 2011). It promotes learning, fosters respect, and engenders bonds among diverse groups of students. A cooperative learning lesson exhibits three basic elements: positive interdependence where responsibility for successful outcomes is shared among all group members; face-to-face opportunities to discuss, ask questions and interact; and, individual accountability. As noted by Johnson, Johnson, and Smith (1991):

  The purpose of cooperative learning groups is to make each member a stronger individual in his or her right. Students learn together so that they can subsequently perform higher as individuals. (p. 67)

- Personalization of Information. Internalizing information is key. The simple premise that the teacher did not teach if the learner did not learn, establishes the quintessential condition for learning. Any student can learn any material at some level of competence by their own volition. Humanistic teachers see themselves as facilitators, assisting their charges in identifying and profiting from their own unique learning styles. The learner's feelings, interest, likes and dislikes, abilities, and other personal qualities are paramount.
- Self-Diagnosis. Learners should be encouraged to share in the responsibility for assessing their own learning. Faculty are charged with offering the learner a variety of opportunities to practice the skills presented in the lesson.

1.2.4. The Constructivist Classroom

Constructivism underscores how learners build knowledge; process is as important as content. Constructivism encourages students to engage in active learning techniques that include experiments, real-world situations, realistic problem-solving, dramatization, etc. If constructivism begins to sound much like cognitivism, that's not a coincidence. There are many constructivist learning activities which lend themselves to the college learning environment.

If you agreed with *statements 13–17* in Appendix A, you favor constructivist learning and use of the following instructional tools.

- Discussion forums – discussion groups and chat rooms – promote faculty and student interaction with face-to-face or online collaboration. An explicit

question or series of questions might serve as the catalyst to increase learning. Students, not teachers, are responsible for exploring, hypothesizing, defending, and communicating their newly acquired knowledge and skills to others in the classroom.
- WebQuests are inquiry-oriented lessons with information required by the learner coming from the web. WebQuests are classroom-based and emphasize higher order thinking skills such as analysis, synthesis, and evaluation rather than the simple acquisition of information (WebQuest Research Consortium, 2016).
- Case-based learning is steeped in the constructivist school of learning. Here, the instructor poses real-world problems using stories. Students are challenged to define, hypothesize, apply, evaluate, and eventually revise possible solutions. Case studies often follow didactic presentations to promote a deeper understanding of the material.

Constructivist teachers promote problem-solving and group work while trying not to direct the conversation. Learners are encouraged to take risks and create their own hypotheses.

1.2.5. The Connectivist Classroom

The newest school of educational psychology offers the paradigm of a computer network to explain learning. Knowledge exists within the larger learning community, and learning occurs when the search for that knowledge triggers connections and networks. Learners are encouraged to participate in lesson-specific discussions using their own networking prowess across multiple platforms such as the personal learning networks (PLNs), differentiated instruction, flipped classrooms, virtual worlds, and a host of technologies.

Statements 18–22 suggest a twenty-first-century vision of learning – one that describes a growing population of learners. Some of the recognized tools of connectivism are examined in the following applications.

- PLNs. Learning with PLNs is not so hard. Some accepted methods include participating in webinars; subscribing to blogs; contributing to other networks rather than simply consuming; sharing one's expertise; creating a wiki, blog, Facebook, LinkedIn, or Twitter account; and attending online conferences and events that focus on personal networks.
- Differentiated Instruction. This lends itself to the principles of connectivism. It encourages teachers to recognize the differences and similarities among their students and use this information to plan instruction so that each student becomes a more accomplished contributor on the larger learning network.

- Flipped Classroom. This is its own movement, especially in higher education where responsibility for learning is shifting from the teacher to the student. Out-of-class assignments are a crucial element in the teaching–learning process. Knowledge previously received face-to-face is supplemented by state-of-the-art technologies such as streaming video and multimedia. Precious classroom time is enhanced with more active student involvement.
- Blended Learning. This aids in the acquisition of knowledge partly by combining classroom instruction and online delivery. It takes the middle ground between traditional and virtual education, alternating between instructional modalities that include distance education, small and large group lessons, whole-class instructions, labs, projects, and one-on-one tutoring. Blended learning is often confused with hybrid learning; there is a subtle distinction. In hybrid learning, a portion of the classes comprising a course is scheduled to take place online. In blended learning, online instruction becomes an integral component of every class session.

1.2.6. Identify a School of Educational Psychology

If you seem to be on the fence between two or more schools, select the school that best describes your learning style. Develop an eclectic style later, as you pursue becoming a master integrator.

Table 1.1 recaps the schools of educational psychology and the key theory, researchers, implications for the classroom, and best practices for higher education.

1.3 TAXONOMIES OF LEARNING

In 1956, Benjamin Bloom, along with his fellow collaborators, Max Engelhart, Edward Furst, Walter Hill, and David Krathwohl, published a framework for classifying educational objectives in an attempt to promote higher forms of thinking. The *Taxonomy of educational objectives*, more commonly known as Bloom's Taxonomy, has been the mainstay of generations of teachers when designing learning.

Bloom's research identified three domains of educational learning objectives. The cognitive domain focuses on mental skills, or knowledge; the affective considers feelings or emotional areas; and the psychomotor domain centers on manual or physical skills. While both the cognitive and the affective domains received the most attention in the 1956 study, it was the cognitive domain that would remain the most widely approved

Table 1.1. Key Characteristics of the Five Schools of Educational Psychology

Component	Behaviorism	Cognitivism	Humanism	Constructivism	Connectivism
Theories	Classical conditioning Connectionism Operant conditioning Social learning theory	Classical cognitivism Stages of cognitive development Zone of proximal development Info processing model Andragogy	Classical humanism Self-actualization Internalization of learning	Classical constructivism Individual constructivism Social constructivism Multiple intelligences Learning transfer model	Classical connectivism Learning networks
Researchers	Pavlov Thorndike Skinner Watson Tolman	Piaget Vygotsky Erikson	Maslow Rogers	Piaget Vygotsky Dewey Bruner Jonassen	Siemens Downes Richardson and Mancabelli
Implications	Instructor feedback Grades Student learning outcomes Behavioral learning objectives	Classroom cognitivism Staying in the zone College student focus Teach toward student engagement	Classroom humanism Freedom to learn Positive communications Personalization of knowledge Self-diagnosis of learning	Classroom constructivism ADDIE model Kemp model Backward design model	Classroom connectivism
Practices	Programmed instruction Computer-assisted instruction Mastery learning Technologies	Discovery learning Andragogy in the college classroom Advanced organizers Technologies	Open education Cooperative learning Technologies	Learning activities Classroom practices Signs of a constructivist classroom Technologies	Learning activities Personal learning networks Whole-class teaching MOOCs Differentiated instruction Flipped classrooms Blended learning Technologies

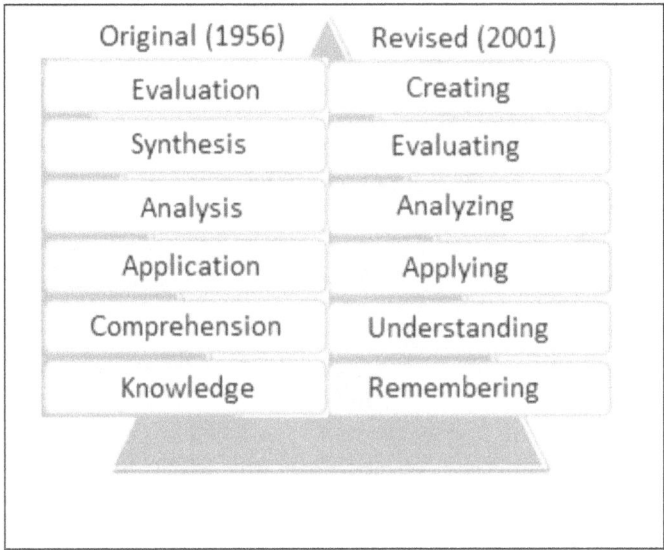

Figure 1.1 Taxonomy of Educational Objectives. *Source*: Author-developed for this book.

and adopted paradigm for constructing knowledge-based learning objectives, starting from the simplest cognitive process or behavior to the most complex.

A group of cognitive psychologists, curriculum theorists, instructional researchers, and testing and assessment specialists published a 2001 revision of Bloom's Taxonomy (Figure 1.1) entitled *A taxonomy for learning, teaching, and assessment* (Anderson & Krathwohl, 2001).

Most educators are familiar with the six major categories of cognitive processes. They include remembering, understanding, applying, analyzing, evaluating, and creating. This text and the Integrated Readiness Matrix use the revised taxonomy for its pedagogical dimension.

Action statements for the taxonomy are provided in Appendix B. They clearly provide criteria for successful learning as well as observable and measurable assessment methodology. The use of action statements assists in providing realistic expectations on the part of students, teachers, and administrators.

1.4. CONCLUSION

Chapter 2 sets the tone for college faculty to develop their pedagogical skills and competencies in the classroom. Key pedagogies of behaviorism, cognitivism, humanism, constructivism, and connectivism were presented, and the taxonomy for the cognitive domain was offered as a theoretical foundation for teaching and learning. Recognizing your own preferred learning style can foster a lifelong growth of these skills to address the learning needs of students.

REFERENCES

Anderson, L. W., & Krathwohl, D. R. (Eds.). (2001). *A taxonomy for learning, teaching, and assessing: A revision of Bloom's taxonomy of educational objectives.* New York: Longman.

Bloom, B. S., Engelhart, M. D., Furst, E. J., Hill, W. H., & Krathwohl, D. R. (Eds.). (1956). *Taxonomy of educational objectives. The classification of educational goals. Handbook I: Cognitive domain.* New York: David McKay.

Brookfield, S. D. (1986). *Understanding and facilitating adult learning: A comprehensive analysis of principles and effective practices.* California: Jossey-Bass.

Johnson, D.W., Johnson, R.T., & Smith, K. A. (1991). *Active learning: Cooperation in the college classroom.* Edina, MN: Interaction.

Karpicke, J. D., & Aue, W. R. (2015). The testing effect is alive and well with complex materials. *Educational Psychology Review*, 27, 317–326. http://learninglab.psych.purdue.edu/publications/.

Knowles, M. S., Swanson, R. A., & Holton, E. F. III (2005). The adult learner: The definitive classic in adult education and human resource development (6th ed.). California: Elsevier Science and Technology Books.

Rosenberg, R. (2013). Quizzes make studying more effective. URL: http://www.uft.org/research-shows/quizzes-make-studying-more-effective.

Slavin, R. E. (2011). Instruction based on cooperative learning. In R. Mayer (Ed.), *Handbook of research on learning and instruction.* London: Taylor & Francis. Instruction Based on Cooperative Learning 09 24 09.pdf.

Slavin, R. E. (1995). *Cooperative learning: Theory, research, and practice* (2nd ed.). Boston: Allyn & Bacon. URL: http://www.pearsonhighered.com/educator/product/Cooperative-Learning-Theory-Research-and-Practice/9780205156306.page.

Smith, M. A., & Karpicke, J. D. (2014). Retrieval practice with short-answer, multiple-choice, and hybrid tests. *Memory*, 22(7), 784–802.

Sockalingam, N. (2012). *Understanding adult learners' needs.* URL: http://www.facultyfocus.com/articles/teaching-and-learning/understanding-adult-learners-needs/.

WebQuest Research Consortium (2016). What is a WebQuest? URL: http://webquest.org/.

Weinstein, Y., Nunes, L. D., & Karpicke, J. D. (2016). On the placement of practice questions during study. *Journal of Experimental Psychology Applied*, 22(1), 72–84.

Chapter 2

Pedagogies of Technology in Higher Education

2.1. INTRODUCTION

In the previous chapter, the schools of behaviorism, cognitivism, humanism, constructivism, and connectivism were introduced. Readers were encouraged to uncover the dominant school with respect to how they learn.

Technology, as arguably the newest school for teaching, addresses the impact and importance of teaching with technology. Many educators view technology as arguably the most important instructional strategy to impact the classroom since the introduction of the printed text. The Taxonomy for the Technology Domain presented here offers an equivalent perspective for teaching commensurate with the other ambits of learning previously discussed.

Research shows that teachers who use a taxonomy to prepare instructional learning objectives tend to produce more successful student learning outcomes (Kibler, Barker, and Miles, 1970; and Krathwohl and Bloom, 1984). The Technology Taxonomy (Figure 2.1) includes literacy, collaboration, decision-making, learning with technology, teaching with technology, and tech-ology. Each step offers a progressively more complex level of thinking by constructing increasingly multifaceted student learning outcomes at each level of activity.

2.2. LITERACY: AT THE BASE OF THE PYRAMID

Technology for literacy represents the most basic level of technology learning. *Literacy* is defined as "the minimum degree of competency expected of teachers and students with respect to technology, computers, educational programs, office productivity software, the Internet, and their synergistic

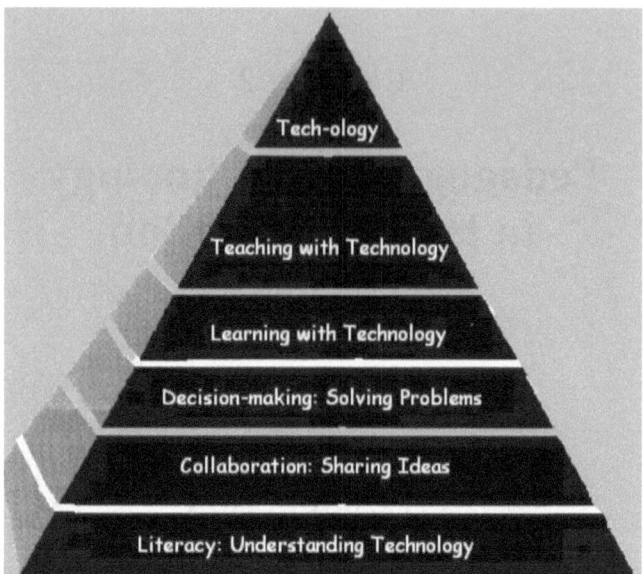

Figure 2.1 Taxonomy for the Technology Domain. *Source*: Tomei, 2005.

effectiveness as a learning strategy" (Tomei, 2005, p. 91). It involves an awareness of technology as a personal tool for learning as well as a content area worthy of mastery in its own right.

2.2.1. Impact of Literacy in Higher Education

For the college teacher, literacy demands a level of skill and competency in the use of technology for personal application. At the outset, the list of required abilities appears daunting. It involves an understanding of technology at its most basic roots; an appreciation of a growing inventory of technological hardware media; and the operation and application of complex operating system, office productivity software, and basic software utilities.

2.2.2. Literacy Technologies and Action Statements

Action statements such as those in Appendix C Table 1 provide clearly stated criteria for successful learning as well as observable and measurable assessment methodology. The use of action statements assist in providing realistic expectations on the part of students, teachers, and administrators.

Literacy raises the bar not only for college students but for faculty as well. To be declared *technology literate*, student or faculty must possess a similar set of skills and competencies. However, the learner can stop there, while the instructor must advance toward the applications of technology in the classroom. Faculty responsibilities demand that they continually grow with emerging technologies and persist in applying these technologies to the classroom. Modeling the use of technology and the personal exercise of hardware and software during instruction is expected.

In addition, the college teacher must attain a level of proficiency in literacy that ensures ongoing professional development and lifelong learning. Literacy pushes the teacher to "continually evaluate and reflect on professional practice to make informed decisions regarding the use of technology in support of student learning" (ISTE, 2002). Literacy involves a plethora of technologies, both high-tech and low-tech. More importantly, these technologies must be selected based upon the cognitive, affective, and psychomotor strategies of the learner.

2.3. COLLABORATION: USING TECHNOLOGY TO SHARE IDEAS

Technology for collaboration is defined as "the ability to employ technology for effective interpersonal interaction" (Tomei, 2005, p. 93). Effective uses of technology include appropriate written and verbal communication, the professional exchange of information, and interpersonal collaboration.

At the second level of the Taxonomy for the Technology Domain, collaboration involves the use of telecommunications to network with peers, teachers, subject-matter experts, and other audiences. Skills at this level of the taxonomy are evidenced by sharing information in written form (e.g., word processing, desktop publishing), by responding to directed personal interchange (e.g., electronic mail), and by participating in and interpreting interpersonal dialog (e.g., list servers, chat rooms, and online bulletin boards).

2.3.1. Impact of Collaboration in Higher Education

To communicate collaboratively, higher education faculty need to know more than simple word processing. They must be able to share ideas by integrating images, sounds, and video into textual content; develop organizational schemata such as graphic organizers, tables of contents, or indexes; and, present ideas in novel formats such as columns, tables, hypertext, and distinctive fonts. Finally, collaboration is evidenced in the synch/asynchronous atmosphere of Internet chat rooms, list servers, and bulletin boards. A new protocol of netiquette has matured from the use of online discussion groups and abbreviated e-mail posts, adding to the historic syntax surrounding the use of correct grammar, mechanics, and spelling.

Perhaps no other level of the taxonomy is as important to successful college teaching as collaboration. In order to enhance productivity and professional practice, ISTE calls upon teachers to use "technology to communicate and collaborate with peers, parents, and the larger community in order to nurture student learning" (ISTE, 2003).

2.3.2. Collaboration Technologies and Action Statements

Appendix C Table 2 offers a list of action verbs and instructional technologies for the second level of the Taxonomy for the Technology Domain.

Collaboration supports the extension of student dialogue far beyond the classroom walls. Higher education faculty, operating at this level of the taxonomy, embrace the use of networks (e.g., Internet, personal learning networks, and digital libraries) as a means to facilitate real-world investigations. Learners share goals, data, findings, analyses, and recommendations without barriers. Those who successfully master this level adapt to the increase in student interaction, and many actually begin to encourage student dialogue outside the classroom experience.

2.4. DECISION-MAKING: SOLVING PROBLEMS

Technology for decision-making refers to the "ability to use technology in new and concrete situations to analyze, assess, and judge" (Tomei, 2005, p. 97). Making decisions with technology requires a greater understanding of technology than either of the previous stages. Decision-making technology includes such important tools as spreadsheets, brainstorming software, statistical analysis packages, and database applications.

Arguably the first software application to justify the purchase of personal computers, spreadsheets represent electronic files in which work and data are stored for manipulation, storage, retrieval, and presentation. Brainstorming software provides the learner with a graphical organizer inherent in creating position papers, plans, strategies, orientations, and technical reports. Statistical packages expand elementary functions that accompany state-of-the-art spreadsheets, including a more comprehensive set of descriptive and inferential statistics. A database is a collection of related information comprised of individual records containing meaningful data captured for later manipulation.

2.4.1. Impact of Decision-Making on Higher Education

Research and problem-solving/decision-making tools comprise strategies for making informed decisions about real-world problems. Decision-making is a key skill in the workplace, and is particularly important for colleges and universities that claim they are preparing workforce-ready graduates.

At this level of the taxonomy, technology can offer tools that help the learner explore and later acquire a number of decision-making skills, including identifying a well-defined process to structure decisions; isolating the real issues before starting a decision-making process; evaluating risks associated with each alternative before making a decision; finding potential solutions to a problem and establishing factors to evaluate those possible solutions; predicting the actual consequences of decisions; sharing data; checking and rechecking assumptions and solutions; promoting group decision-making; and many others.

2.4.2. Decision-Making Technologies and Action Statements

Collectively, the action statements in Appendix C Table 3 offer a comparative handful of decision-making technologies for consideration.

Decision-making technologies in the higher education classroom offer options and alternatives upon which to base decisions and advance a higher degree of personal and professional involvement. They promote information gathering, summarize possible conclusions, identify possible alternatives, and uncover the most desirable courses of action. These technologies monitor the effectiveness of the decision-making process – important skills for the affective domain of teaching.

2.5. LEARNING WITH TECHNOLOGY: INFUSING TECHNOLOGY INTO THE LEARNING PROCESS

Learning with technology recognizes technology as a powerful strategy for uncovering and exploring academic content. At this level, faculty are concerned with the "identification, harvesting, and applications of existing technology to unique learning situations" (Tomei, 2005, p. 100). Here, teachers and learners move from the external use of technology to solve problems to an internal application of technology to learning in general. The educational value of available materials is considered as technology-based resources are selected for instruction and individualized learning. Infusion is found in printed, audio, visual, multimedia, and web-based technologies in addition to the more predictable categories of educational hardware, software, and networking.

The potential for using different technologies to facilitate the learning process is virtually unlimited. Technologies make it possible to visualize problems formerly confined to printed text and link with diverse learning communities usually restricted to the traditional classroom. Infused technologies simulate new worlds that simply do not exist except in the imagination and fosters student participation in learning goals once thought too dangerous and too costly.

2.5.1. Impact of Learning with Technology in Higher Education

For instruction at this level of the taxonomy to be effective, technology must be infused into the curriculum and not allowed to serve merely as remedial or enrichment instruction. Technologies, offered by a knowledgeable instructor, maximize student learning options, address the diverse needs of individual students, develop their higher order thinking skills, and contribute to stronger academic content throughout the curriculum. For technology to be effective at this level, college faculty must determine when technology tools can be most useful and how they can address the multiplicity of tasks and problems that will be encountered by the learner over a lifetime.

The teacher must ensure that learners are aware of their learning styles and how infused technology can strengthen their own learning goals. An excellent example is the proliferation of educational software as infused technology. While every teacher seeks to introduce appropriate educational software (e.g., demonstration, freeware, or shareware) at suitable points within the curriculum, it is the conscientious teacher who also provides a venue for self-evaluation of related software apart from the safety of the classroom. Managing the infusion of technology into student learning activities provides the learner with opportunities for selecting among a growing inventory of lifelong learning materials.

2.5.2. Learning Technologies and Action Statements

Appendix C Table 4 exhibits common action verbs for this level of the Taxonomy for the Technology Domain.

Teachers use technology to provide instructional materials previously unavailable. By locating new classroom materials (most of which is digital in format), they select from among a growing inventory of text, visual, and web-based resources focused on the learning styles of students and augmented by their own particular teaching strategy.

2.6. TEACHING WITH TECHNOLOGY: INTEGRATING TEACHER-MADE RESOURCES INTO THE CURRICULUM

Teaching with Technology "is concerned with the creation of new technology-based materials, combining otherwise disparate technologies to teach"

(Tomei, 2005, pg 103). The objective is to develop new, previously nonexistent, innovative instructional materials to enhance learner understanding. Appropriate technology-based components are assembled to a degree not previously possible with textbooks, audiovisuals, or copied materials.

2.6.1. Impact of Teaching with Technology in Higher Education

Integration occurs as faculty endeavor to compose their own content-specific resources using technologies mastered at the previous levels of the taxonomy. Integration demands significantly more skill. In point of fact, integration is the most mature application of technology. At this level, faculty are asked to design, develop, implement, and deliver developmentally appropriate instructional materials to support a more diverse inventory of learning styles. To accomplish this feat, faculty must be able to apply the most contemporary research with current technologies when planning learning environments and experiences (ISTE, 2003). Simply put, faculty must move technology beyond classroom presentations to prepare resources that are appropriate for student-centered instruction.

2.6.2. Teaching Technologies and Action Statements

Table 5 in Appendix C presents possible action statements for students, teachers, and administrators.

Text, visual, and web-based resources are within the reach of any teacher equipped with multimedia computers, office productivity software, and access to the Internet. Text-based handouts, study guides, and worksheets are prepared using images and text harvested from the web and created using word processing. Visual-based lessons address the demands of the visual learner by using harvested images, sounds, text, and video integrated into a class presentation. Web-based home pages, prepared with state-of-the-art editors, reduce the risk of unsupervised Internet exploration while focusing attention on validated content-area sites.

2.7. TECH-OLOGY: THE STUDY OF TECHNOLOGY

The final level of the technology taxonomy is "the ability to judge the universal impact, shared values, and social implications of technology use and its influence on teaching and learning" (Tomei, 2005, pg 106). *Tech-ology* is a contraction of *tech* (technology) and *ology* (the study of); therefore, this stage addresses the study of technology. Many related issues necessarily come to the front when considering the effect of technology on the individual learner, the educational institution, the community, and society as a whole.

2.7.1. Impact of Tech-ology in Higher Education

In addition to education and the basic technology issues, tech-ology is impacted by social and issues such as equity matters, economic innovations, and national security fears, such as cyber-warfare, information security abuses, and terrorism. Personal security is in the news with the technology-induced cyber-stalking, insider trading and other illegal business practices, censorship on the Internet, as well as the more traditional issues of personal privacy, identity theft, and home safety.

2.7.2. Tech-ology Technologies and Action Statements

Tech-ology serves to expand on important cultural issues. Use of the various technologies shown in Appendix C Table 6 promote individual thinking and, as a result, entail a more sophisticated level of understanding from students, teachers, and administrators.

2.8. CONCLUSIONS

New technologies continue to evolve, challenging current thinking, policy, and practice. Virtual field trips, unimagined only a few short years ago, enable students to visit cultural and educational sites around the world without ever leaving their classroom. Educational websites, now numbering into the millions, steer educators to resources that help with lesson-plan design and personal professional development. Authors of these sites often employ as many technologies as possible to address the range of learning styles and teaching strategies encountered in today's diverse classrooms. Teachers and learners tap into videoconferencing resources, satellite content providers, and online and web-based services for their news, sports, biographies and history, travel, entertainment, as well as academic content. The truly exciting aspect of using technologies for teaching and learning is to consider the *dynamic interplay of technology with culture and society*.

REFERENCES

International Society for Technology in Education (ISTE), *Educational Technology Standards and Performance Indicators for All Teachers*, National Educational

Technology Standards for Teachers. URL: cnets.iste.org/teachers/t_stands.html, 2003.

Kibler, R.J., Barker, L.L., and Miles, D.T. (1970). Behavioral objectives and instruction. New York: Allyn & Bacon/Longman/Pearson Publishers.

Krathwohl, D.L. and Bloom, Benjamin S. (1984). Taxonomy of educational objectives. the classifications of educational goals. Handbook I. New York: Addison-Wesley Company/Pearson Publishers.

Tomei, Lawrence A. Taxonomy for the Technology Domain: A Classification of Educational Objectives for the Technology Domain, Idea Group Publishers, Inc. 2005.

Part II

THE CULTURAL INFLUENCES OF ORGANIZATIONS

Part Two describes both the cultural influences that surround all organizations, including higher education. This part also explores those influences that impede organizational change in general and in higher education specifically. Chapter 3 offers a perspective regarding the cultural influences on organizations and the individuals that work in these organizations based on Urie Bronfenbrenner's Ecological Systems Theory. Chapter 4 looks more explicitly at the culture of higher education and the factors that influence the successful integration of the Integrated Readiness Matrix (IRM) into a Center for Teaching Excellence. The purpose of this entire part is to provide a foundation for understanding and interpreting the real-time development of a center for teaching excellence and the introduction of the IRM.

Because this book was written as the Robert Morris University's Center for Innovative Teaching and Directed Engaged Learning was still undergoing development at Robert Morris University under the pilot introduction of the IRM, this chapter served both as a guide during implementation during the fall 2015 semester and as a source of reflection following the first year of implementation. In this sense, we are both doing and learning, and hopefully this dual undertaking will prove useful to those who want to develop an effective way to promote ongoing professional development in their own institutions of higher education. In essence, we hope to make a case for promoting lifelong faculty development based on arguments that favor a Center for Teaching Excellence with the IRM as the primary development tool.

Chapter 3

The Culture of Organizations

3.1. INTRODUCTION

Although higher education has unique cultural features, it shares many characteristics with other types of organizations; higher education is, after all, a business albeit one specializing in the *production* of knowledge. This chapter therefore begins by advancing a perspective on those influences that are continuously yet invisibly shaping individuals, organizational structures, and decision-making.

It also assumes that there are similarities in terms of impediments and challenges that face those who wish to suggest organizational changes that are more visible and proactive whether in higher education or other types of organizations. Resistance to change seems to be an inherent feature of both individuals and the organizations in which they reside, even if such change is generally recognized as a healthy ingredient for organizational well-being and success.

Urie Bronfenbrenner (1989) introduced his *Ecological Systems Theory* which later blossomed into the *Bioecological Model of Human Development* (Bronfenbrenner & Morris, 2006). This theoretical model sees the individual as surrounded by influences represented by concentric circles (see Figure 3.1).

While our interpretation of this model focuses on organizations as well as individuals and will center specifically on the development of a Center for Teaching Excellence in higher education and integration of the Integrated Readiness Matrix (IRM), it is important to recognize influences on the individual within this more general and contextual organizational framework. The influences described in this model include those exerted by home and family in the *Microsystem* that have a more direct and immediate influence

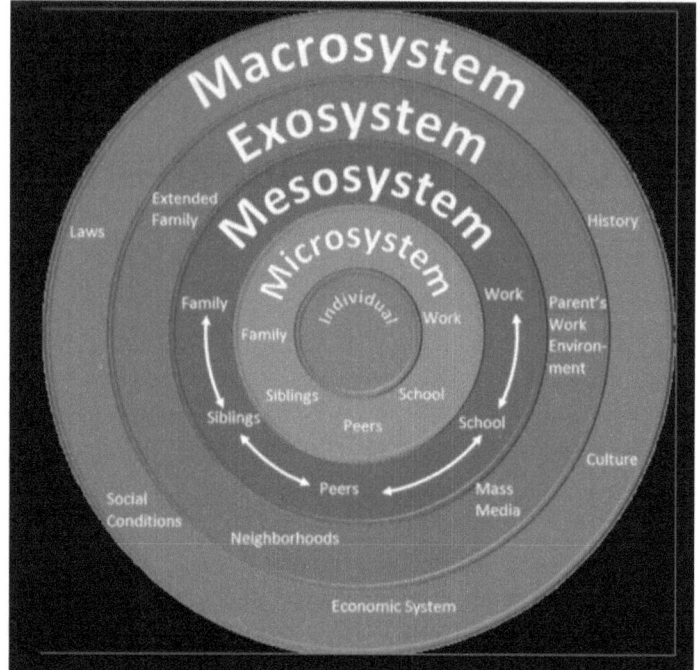

Figure 3.1 The Bioecological Model. *Source:* Bronfenbrenner, 1989.

on individuals than do those influencers farther removed in the Meso-, Exo-, and Macrosystems. However, not only are there hypothesized reciprocal influences among these different systems, there are also oscillating influences *within* each system, such as among school, work, and peers in the Mesosystem.

The assumed reciprocal interaction among these layers of the model seems to make provision for the potential of individuals to exert counterinfluences that are quite desirable from the perspective of the need for individuals to perceive some degree of self-efficacy rather than powerlessness in order to foster healthy human development and learning.

In addition, the influence of the specific *time period* is also said to influence all development – the *chronosystem*. We will see how the time period affects organizations when we discuss the relationship among Baby Boomers, Gen Xers, and Millennials below.

Notwithstanding the implied provision of the Bioecological Model for recognizing the possibility of individual and organizational resistance or *pushback*, there is also an undeniable social and cultural influence on both individuals and organizations that can be likened in some way to the air that we daily inhale and exhale including its ambient temperature and humidity.

While we are sometimes consciously aware of our breathing and the quality of the air that surrounds us, for the most part we are like fish in the ocean as we unconsciously go about our lives within our own *ocean* of air. The influences of Bronfenbrenner's *systems* on us and the way we unconsciously go about our lives within the *air* of organizations incorporate tacit acceptance of expectations of *how things are done* in our own organizations. When we focus on higher education in the next chapter, it will be helpful to remember this model so that we are armed with a more complete conception of the context within which we function in higher education.

3.2. THE CULTURE OF ORGANIZATIONS

Organizations are mankind's way to effect control and change within a powerful societal milieu as illustrated by the *Bioecological Model of Human Development*. What should financial organizations look like to help us save and borrow money and keep commerce and the economy flowing? What about governmental organizations? Religious organizations? K-12 schooling? What expectations and pressures influence these organizations as they go about trying to achieve their missions?

In other words, what kind of culture is developing or evolving (depending on one's perspective) in these organizations in response to societal cultural influences, and what are their impacts on the individuals within these organizations as well as individuals' impacts on the organization? While we cannot provide an exhaustive explanation, we can highlight some general considerations that include the effects of *competition, development of organizations, impediments to change, the impact of technology, generational labels, and moving forward._*These considerations are extended into the next chapter for further discussion of the unique culture of higher education.

3.3. EFFECTS OF COMPETITION

Organizations as well as individuals must compete in order to survive and prosper. Whether such competition is global, national, regional, local, or a combination of levels, there is ongoing competition for raw resources, financial resources, and human resources. Competition demands that organizations remain aware of changes in their marketplace and adapt to changing conditions and expectations. The ideas discussed earlier by Melcher (1976) and Weick (2001) as well as the Bioecological Model can be interpreted through the lens of competition. Competition is an ever present influence on behavior and decision-making.

Porter (1980) described a framework for understanding competition and argued that there are five types of *opponents* that range from direct competitors to buyers and suppliers. It may seem odd that buyers are considered competitive opponents since they are in fact the consumers of products and services that are produced. However, the argument is that customers exercise power over organizations to the extent that they have the freedom to buy products and services from other companies that offer lower prices. This same competitive pressure is described in the next chapter regarding higher education.

In addition, organizations can realize a *competitive advantage,* defined as "the value a firm is able to create in excess of (accounting and opportunity) costs" (Wilson, J.O.S, 2008, p. 220). The creation of excess value includes physical, monetary, and perceptual value. It is often value *as perceived* by customers that results in individuals deciding to purchase goods and services from particular organizations. Reputation and other intangibles are the reason why organizations are so focused on *branding* and zealously defend against encroachment by competitors.

Because of advances in technology, communication, and the ease of transportation, we are engaged more than ever in global as well as regional competition. Activities such as strategic planning and the involvement and engagement of the members of the organization in planning can have a tremendous impact on the success of organizations dealing with competition within the milieu of social and cultural influences. Bartunek, Austin, and Seo (2008) note that "business environments have become increasingly global, competitive, and turbulent, forcing many companies to rethink their purposes and directions" (p. 159). It can be safely assumed that *all* organizations to varying degrees function within this transformed environment. The Bioecological Model in Figure 3.1 is extended not only in terms of the time dimension but also in relation to the diffuse influences of competition.

While government regulation is not generally considered as competition, the Bioecological Model addresses laws and the economic system as critical components of the Macrosystem that exerts influence on both individuals and organizations. While laws and regulations are presumably put into place to provide for the common good, there is no question that they consume valuable resources including time, treasure, and expertise. The wise organization transforms regulations into opportunities for improving their competitive position.

As Miles and Snow (1978) point out, one of the differences between effective and ineffective organizations is that the former "constantly modify and refine the mechanism by which they achieve their purpose – rearranging their structure of roles and relationships and their decision-making and control processes" (p. 3) while the latter organizations fail to do so. It is the ability of organizations to learn and develop and to promote the learning and growth of its members that enables these organizations to thrive rather than simply survive.

3.4. ORGANIZATIONAL DEVELOPMENT

The field of organizational development (OD) began about 1958 in response to organizational challenges and evolved into a methodology for helping organizations cope with rapid changes posed both by cultural influences and by global competition. Burke (2008) also makes a direct connection between organizational and professional development, making the case that "because OD is a field of study and practice rather than a profession, choices for education and professional development are not clear-cut" (p. 20). Education is also referred to as a *field of study* rather than a profession, while professional development is often called *training* when it focuses more on core business practices rather than the development of the potential of individuals.

Argyris (2008) strongly advocates that organizations need to be places for learning as well as for production: "I begin with the premise that learning is key to effective organizational change and development" (p. 53). He goes on to point out that leaders often voice the value of employee and staff development, yet formal and informal power grabs often preclude subordinates from being honest or creative. Leaders are judged by the impact that they have on growing and improving the organization. Strong leaders often generate unintended consequences, silencing the voices of those who may have problems or opportunities.

Argyris (1999) also explored the defensive forces that inhibit organizational learning. Inhibitors to organizational learning parallel inhibitors to change in organizations generally. However, perhaps one of the most insightful observations that Argyris makes is the double-edged sword that *tacit knowledge* has on effective management and leadership. Argyris does not explicitly cite Polanyi (1962) when he discusses tacit knowledge, best described as knowledge developed from sources such as apprehensions, intuition, and feelings; however, he contrasts this type of knowledge with propositional knowledge that can be described and communicated more easily through language.

Argyris points out that while tacit knowledge is fundamental for effective leadership and management, it carries within it the seeds of deterioration. Tacit knowledge is often limited to solving problems as they currently exist in the organization. The net effect is that tacit knowledge becomes an impediment to developing a culture that values inquiry and creative thinking to address *future* problems and opportunities. The result is that the status quo is reinforced. Thinking back to the Bioecological Model, it is easy to see how the battle lines are constantly shifting – change versus the status quo engages participants in a contest that is often played out invisibly and below the surface of what transpires in organizations on a daily basis.

Senge (2006) has also long espoused the importance of the *learning organization*, where the emphasis is both on actions that can create new organizational realities and on systems thinking that emphasizes integrating across diverse fields in order to see reality as a whole rather than as isolated snapshots. Senge refers to systems thinking as the fifth discipline "because it is the conceptual cornerstone that underlies all of the five learning disciplines" (p. 69). Systems thinking enables us to see "interrelationships rather than things" (p. 68) and how these interrelationships help us cope successfully with the ever-growing complexity of not only social and global problems but also the exponential growth of information.

Senge (2006) reminds us that a learning organization is needed in order to equip us to synthesize and see patterns among the myriad data and influences that continuously impinge on our ability to make sense of the environment. And, making sense of our environment is needed in order to continuously grow and adapt both individually and organizationally in order to proactively transform the environment rather than simply adapt to it.

3.5. IMPEDIMENTS TO CHANGE IN ORGANIZATIONS

Invisible forces of social change led to the evolution of the field of OD and the concept of the learning organization. The inevitability of change is all-encompassing and yet individuals and organizations continue to embrace stability and equilibrium and exhibit a natural aversion to environments that are perceived as unstable and threatening. Whether we are confronted with changes that occur in our churches, political structure, or the organizations in which we work, there is a natural inertia that wants to keep us rooted in the culture that we know.

Argyris (1999), when describing a case involving Intel, links the uncertainty of top management regarding a problem to a manifestation of resistance to change (p. 28). While this case is more complex than the dyad of uncertainty leading to resistance to change, it is worthwhile to consider this hypothesized causal relationship in relation to individuals and organizations including higher education. Although the predilections of entities can certainly vary, is it not often the case that when things are not clear to us that the safest choice is to continue pursuing the same course of action? Some might endorse this mindset and approach, others might perceive this response to uncertainty by using the metaphor of *putting one's head in the sand*.

Argyris (1999) goes on to say that *defensive reasoning* can be manifested when managers believe that "it is better to fail with existing procedures than to fail trying something new, especially when business is [*deleted quote mark*] okay and no one is really up against the wall" (p. 39). Often, inertia and desire for equilibrium militate against individuals and organizations embracing creative and proactive initiatives.

Piaget (1954) described the equilibrium–disequilibrium tug-of-war that occurs within individuals when what once made sense no longer works in light of new realities and new problems. However, it is only when we experience this *disequilibrium* that we discover the necessity or incentive to grow. While Piaget was concerned with individual growth and development, the notion of disequilibrium extends to the organization. We are faced both in our personal lives and in our organizational lives with the choice of how to perceive the inevitable changes that present themselves. Yet, like an oyster experiencing the irritation of sand to produce a pearl, so too do the unwanted influences that are thrust upon us sometimes result in more positive outcomes for the organizations we inhabit.

Senge (1990) asks rhetorically, "who could resist the benefits of personal mastery?" (p. 135). He suggests that both people and organizations regularly exhibit resistance that manifests itself by categorizing the whole concept of *personal mastery* as a soft skill that seems to be akin to the type of knowledge that Polanyi (1962) refers to as *tacit knowledge*. Could it be that a reluctance or refusal to acknowledge the value of this kind of knowledge results in an organizational culture in which individuals feel that it is too risky to go out on a limb by suggesting new approaches based on their own unique perspectives to propose new opportunities that exist for growth?

3.6. TECHNOLOGY

Technology is sometimes met with enthusiasm, other times with resistance. Counts (1961) discussed the *profound change* that our civilization experienced during the 1940s and 1950s in terms of tools used on both farm and factory and the consequent impacts that these changes continue to have on the way we work and live. As we write these words in the year 2016, we recognize that commentators from earlier generations would be utterly astounded at the technological impact that we experience virtually every minute of every day. Vygotsky (1978) was one of the earliest theorists who recognized the influence of technology on learning. Few could have imagined the impact of twenty-first-century tools from computers, smart boards, and personal devices to the ubiquitous smart phone.

However, while most people embrace technological changes that allow them to enjoy their personal and social lives to a fuller extent, technology can present other problems, forcing us to solve these problems in new and innovative ways. The term *Luddites* was originally used to identify workers in early nineteenth-century England who destroyed machinery because of its perceived negative impact on employment. Today, the term is used to identify those people who push back against technology because of a perceived host of more far-reaching drawbacks.

We are all current witnesses to the continuing impact of technology on transportation, commerce, and medicine to name a few. There is simply no denying its significance. Of particular importance to this text is how technology can be positioned in higher education as an opportunity for personal and organizational growth as discussed in the next chapter.

3.7. GENERATIONAL LABELS

While technology is an important barometer of individual variation, some would argue that it is the readiness to use technology that is an indicator of willingness to change. As described earlier, the *chronosystem* of the Bioecological Model (Figure 4.1) refers to the element of time and time periods. While the phrase *the greatest generation* has been used to refer to those persons who were born prior to World War II and participated in the defeat of the Axis powers, the very phrase applied to this generation bespeaks honor and respect. However, when we come to discuss the generations and cohorts of individuals born after World War II, the terms that are used, while not derogatory, certainly do not convey such laudatory connotations.

Baby Boomers typically refer to individuals born between the years 1946 and 1965; *Gen Xers* refer to those born after 1965 but before 1980; and *Millennials* refer to individuals born in the 1980s or 1990s. Attributions are sometimes made based on these demarcations. For example, Baby Boomers are the *go-between* generation and are often regarded as the generation that has undergone the most change. Early boomers found themselves sandwiched between the Greatest Generation of the 1940s and unpopular wars, technological marvels, and the turbulent 1960s.

The Gen Xers have also experienced much social and technological change. While they have not grown up with cell phones or the *apps* that have transformed smart phones into something infinitely more complex and powerful, both Baby Boomers and Gen Xers have made these technologies pervasive.

Millennials are the first generation of *digital natives*. In a recent news article (Fleisher, 2015), Millennials were found to favor open spaces, a team approach, even greater reliance on technology, and flexibility in work arrangements (p. E1). These characteristics seem to convey a growing willingness to embrace higher degrees of change and grander embrace of technology in the workplace.

The mixture of Baby Boomers, Gen Xers, and Millennials in organizations and, as we will see in the next chapter, higher education, presents both opportunities and challenges to those who wish to successfully manage change.

3.8. MOVING FORWARD

Resistance to change is a well-known and accepted concept often used as an excuse for not taking risks or proposing new and creative strategies. Ford and Ford (2010) explore why resistance to change should be looked at not from a defensive position or as a rationalization for inaction but rather as an integral component for formulating effective change strategy. They describe a scenario where three managers interpret the results of meetings with employees whose purpose was to inform these employees about upcoming procedural changes in the organization. One manager reported significant push back. Another described stonewalling. The third manager recounted finding a receptive audience while reporting that "overall it was an engaging and energizing meeting. Nothing like what happened to you two" (p. 25).

Ford and Ford (2010) point out that the real issue is how individuals perceive resistance to change. While the first manager interpreted too many questions as resistance, the second manager interpreted a lack of questions as resistance. However, the third manager interpreted neither the presence nor the absence of questions as resistance but rather as a portal for further discussion and opportunity to move forward.

Perceptions can exert a strong influence on the ultimate success of change efforts and growth strategies. It is not only the objective features of organizational leadership change efforts that matter, it is also those features more akin to *soft skills* that determine the degree to which employees ultimately accept change. We will discuss this issue further in the next chapter when we focus on higher education.

REFERENCES

Argyris, C. (1999). *On Organizational learning* (2nd ed.). Malden, MA: Blackwell Publishers Inc.

Argyris, C. (2008). Learning in organizations. In T.G. Cummings (Ed.), *Handbook of organizational development* (pp. 53–67). Los Angeles, CA: SAGE Publications.

Bartunek, J. M., Austin, J. R., & Gu-Seo, M. (2008). Conceptual underpinnings of intervening in organizations. In T.G. Cummings (Ed.), *Handbook of organizational development* (pp. 151–166). Los Angeles, CA: SAGE Publications.

Bronfenbrenner, U. (1989). Ecological systems theory. In R. Vasta (Ed.), *Annals of child development* (Vol. 6, pp. 187–249). Boston, MA: JAI Press Inc.

Bronfenbrenner, U. & Morris, P. A. (2006). The bioecological model of human development. In W. Damon & R.M. Lerner (Eds.), *Handbook of child psychology: Theoretical models of human development* (6th ed., Vol. 1, pp. 793–827). Hoboken, NJ: Wiley.

Burke, W. W. (2008). A contemporary view of organizational development. In T. G. Cummings (Ed.), *Handbook of organizational development* (pp. 13–38). Los Angeles, CA: SAGE Publications.

Counts, G. (1961). The impact of technological change. In W. G. Bennes, K. D. Benne & R. Chin (Eds.), *The planning of change* (pp. 20–28). New York, NY: Holt, Rinehart, and Winston.

Dupuis, J.P. (2008). Organizational culture. In S. R. Clegg & J. R. Bailey (Eds.), *International Encyclopedia of Organization Studies* (pp. 1035–1039). Los Angeles, CA: SAGE Publications.

Fleisher, C. (2015, November 1). Millennial input shapes workplaces. *Pittsburgh Tribune-Review*, pp. E1, E6.

Ford, J. D. & Ford, L. W. (2010). Stop blaming resistance to change and start using it. *Organizational Dynamics, 39*(1), 24–35.

Hall, G. E., & Hord, S. M. (1987). *Change in schools: Facilitating the process.* Albany, NY: State University of New York Press.

Melcher, A. J. (1976). *Structure and process of organizations: A systems approach.* Englewood Cliffs, NJ: Prentice-Hall Inc.

Miles, R. E. & Snow, C. C. (1978). *Organizational strategy, structure, and process.* New York, NY: McGraw-Hill Book Company.

Mohr, J. W. (2008). Cultural Capital. In S. R. Clegg & J. R. Bailey (Eds.), *International Encyclopedia of Organization Studies* (pp. 343–345). Los Angeles, CA: SAGE Publications.

Piaget, J. (1954). *The construction of reality in the child* (M. Cook, Trans.). New York, NY: Basic Books.

Pinkham, B. C., Picken, J. C., & Dess, G. G. (2010). The role of leveraging technology. *Organizational Dynamics, 39*(3), 226–239.

Polanyi, M. (1962). *Personal knowledge: Towards a post-critical philosophy.* Chicago, IL: The University of Chicago Press.

Porter, M. E. (1980). Competitive strategy: Techniques for analyzing industries and competitors. New York, NY: Free Press.

Senge, P. M. (2006). The fifth discipline. The art and practice of the learning organization. New York, NY: Currency Doubleday.

Vygotsky, L. S. (1978). *Mind in society: The development of higher mental process.* Cambridge, MA: Harvard University Press.

Weick, K. E. (2001). *Making sense of the organization.* Malden, MA: Blackwell Publishing.

Wertsch, J. V. (1991). *Voices of the mind: A sociocultural approach to mediated action.* Cambridge, MA: Harvard University Press.

Wilson, J. O. S. (2008). Competitive advantage. In S. R. Clegg & J. R. Bailey (Eds.), *International Encyclopedia of Organization Studies* (pp. 220–223). Los Angeles, CA: SAGE Publications.

Chapter 4

The Culture of Higher Education

4.1. INTRODUCTION

This chapter focuses on higher education, building upon the previous chapter regarding organizations in general. In this chapter, we follow a similar outline emphasizing aspects of higher education culture, effects of competition, development of higher education, impediments to change, impact of technology, generational labels, and moving forward that are unique to higher education.

This chapter examines the similarities and differences between higher education and other types of organizations. Of special interest are the unique characteristics of governance and academic freedom that exist in higher education – all factors to be considered when developing a Center for Teaching Excellence and implementing a professional development system based on the Integrated Readiness Matrix (IRM).

The authors highlight the unique challenges to change in higher education. Core functions of teaching and learning are introduced along with specific challenges associated with ongoing pedagogical development (how we teach) versus the diversity of academic content (what we teach) found in higher education. The chapter describes how research, teaching, and service can be strengthened and promoted by using the IRM as an instrument of change.

4.2. THE CULTURE OF HIGHER EDUCATION

Higher education, because it is first an organization, shares many of the social and cultural characteristics of any organization. Faculty and staff, plants and facilities, technology, offices, and the realization of diminishing budgets characterize the typical university campus. In addition, many of the same social and cultural influences regularly impact both the university environment and the people that work in it. The Bioecological Model (refer again to chapter 3, Fig. 3.1) provides a framework for all organizations. Higher education shares many of the same characteristics and therefore is subject to many of the same influences on faculty and staff. However, there are also very distinct differences between higher education and other organizations.

For those who have worked in both corporate and higher education environments, these differences are readily apparent. Issues as deep and fundamental as academic freedom and less weightier concerns such as dress code speak directly to the unique attributes of the higher education environment.

The literature is replete with features of organizational structure in higher education that definitely differentiate it from other organizations. In the interest of time, we will restrict the discussion to those social and cultural influences that most promote or impede integrating the IRM into a Center for Teaching Excellence.

Tierney (2008) focuses on differences among higher education organizations in terms of their objective versus enacted environments – between those who see reality as fixed and rational and those who prefer the lens of constructivism to describe an individualistic understanding of reality. From a research perspective, opposing views of reality were described eloquently by Gage (1989) when he projected an imaginary journey beyond 1989 to 2009, ending with a reminder that students and not our preferred paradigms should matter most.

Tierney (2008) picks up on the theme when he points out that from both a research and practice perspective, ideal versions of either approach rarely exist and that most endeavors occur along a broad continuum (p. 13). In addition, Tierney offers a diagnostic tool for understanding the culture of higher education so that problems can be identified and resolved. His "working framework" suggests that we investigate the culture of a particular higher education organization in terms of its environment, mission, socialization, information, strategy, and leadership (Tierney, 2008, Table 3.1, p. 30). The authors have incorporated this framework as part of our own strategy when implementing a Center for Teaching Excellence with the IRM as its model. We will explain how in the chapters that follow.

Tierney (2008) also discusses the "disciplinary view of generating knowledge" where the academic discipline is seen as the primary shaper of academic life (p. 50.). Here, teaching and research, especially as it relates to ongoing professional development, is most relevant when integrating the IRM into Centers of Teaching Excellence. We agree with Tierney that the production of new knowledge is socially constructed and that "disciplines are continually reconstituted and reconstructed" (p. 52).

As we go about trying to establish a Center for Teaching Excellence using the IRM model, we see learning as an ongoing conversation not only within academic disciplines but among and between faculties as they learn, share, adapt, and modify pedagogical practices. Professional development for faculty in higher education is a proposition with multiple points of interaction among content, practice, and the professionals both within and outside specific disciplines.

Weick (1983) applies the phrase *loosely coupled* to educational organizations to convey that while individuals may be seemingly attached in terms of purpose and actions, such attachments "may be circumscribed, infrequent, weak, in its mutual affects, unimportant, and/or slow to respond" (p. 18). Weick also stresses that individuals in educational organizations tend to "over-rationalize their activities and to attribute greater meaning, predictability, and coupling among them than in fact they have" (p. 26). For those working in higher education, it is difficult not to see evidence of *loose coupling* and *over-rationalization* in action!

Colleges and universities incorporate the typical components of organizations such as accounting, auditing, purchasing, security, and physical plant operations in order to operate successfully in the real world. However, a more complex, interrelated phenomena of teaching and scholarly inquiry coupled with highly educated professionals can better explain the *disconnects* seen in university life as often conveyed by the metaphor of *herding cats*. Articulated by Weick more than 30 years ago, they remain relevant for higher education.

Lastly, Baldridge (1983) focused more directly on higher education rather than educational organizations in general and sought to depict its structure by invoking an image of "organized anarchy" (pp. 43–45). A fitting complement to Weick's (1983) description of educational organizations as both loosely coupled and over-rationalized, Baldridge lists several key characteristics including lack of clear goals, clients who impact decision-making, and complex or problematic technology. Based on these characteristics, he categorizes higher education as a professionalized organization where "professionals serving the clients demand a large measure of control over the institution's decision processes" (p. 43).

While clients include other organizations (e.g., government agencies), for those who teach in higher education, what comes first to mind are students. Scholarly inquiry and research are obviously important endeavors for faculty (especially in large research universities). Yet, few universities could exist without their core clients. In fact, we suspect that both students and parents would be quite surprised to learn that teaching and learning sometimes take a back seat to scholarship as a criterion for promotion and tenure.

4.3. EFFECTS OF COMPETITION

The Bioecological Model (Fig. 4.1) clearly illustrates the social, political, and economic influences that impact both individuals and organizations. While the metrics of market share and profitability are generally not employed in the nonprofit world (including higher education), there is no question that higher education organizations spend a great deal of time and resources on recruitment, retention, and finances.

Higher education embraces the term *knowledge production* rather than *knowledge construction*. The essential mission of colleges and universities is not only to discover new knowledge, but to relate and apply that knowledge to previously accepted and adopted concepts and disciplines. Similar to other organizations, higher education does have its competitors (i.e., sister institutions) and its customers (e.g., students and foundations) (Porter, 1980). While higher education generally manages to coexist within a particular market niche, continuous reevaluation is necessary due to the relentless influences of competition. Strategic planning and the educational mission of higher education must remain sensitive to these influences – just like other public organizations.

One area of competition that is of special concern to higher education is the quality of its faculty. The long-term impact of faculty scholarship and teaching excellence on the reputation of higher education cannot be underestimated. The marketing of academic achievements is an essential function of universities since students and resources depend on the extent that important constituencies outside of the university are aware of its accomplishments. This text provides a model for creating the capacity for faculty to continuously learn and grow within our university community by developing a Center for Teaching Excellence utilizing the IRM.

4.4. PROFESSIONAL DEVELOPMENT

In the previous chapter, we discussed organizational development. We focus now on its counterpart, professional development, in higher education. The evolution of these two quasi-parallel approaches to learning differs primarily due to the nature of the core skills and competencies that characterize them.

While OD developed as a response to common cultural and competitive influences, professional development in educational organizations varies based on the level of education. For Pre-12 schools in the United States, teachers must attain both initial certification and ongoing credentialing via sanctioned experiences and coursework in order to practice their profession.

Although there are variations by state, this focus on externally imposed ongoing certification is similar to what is found in many professions including medicine, insurance, engineering, and finance.

In higher education, there is a noted absence of requirements regarding credentialing for its faculty. However, universities often voluntarily join professional organizations and submit themselves to a regulated credentialing process as evidence of both legitimacy and quality. Faculty members are hired primarily based on a terminal degree (usually a doctorate) plus successful scholarship in their discipline. There are no certifications per se as in Pre-12 education. The culture of higher education regards candidates and practicing faculty as intrinsically motivated toward scholarly pursuits on the ladder from assistant to associate to full professor. Unlike organizations, there are two essential points to note here. First, the process in higher education is voluntary – for now, there are few externally imposed government mandates. Second, its focus is primarily on service and scholarship with effective teaching as given at most institutions.

Bain (2004) when reflecting on how he prepared to teach his first college-level class in US history, relates "I scribbled four questions on the back of an envelope. Years later I found that scrap of my youthful self tucked in an old notebook and discovered that my needs were apparently simple: Where's the classroom? What textbook will I use? What will I include in my lectures? How many tests will I give?" (p. 48). He goes on to relate his current conversations with faculty whom when asked what they would do if courses did not already exist and they could develop their own courses found similarities across faculty and disciplines.

These similarities "stemmed from a deeper base, from primary conceptions of what it means to teach and learn and then shaped the way they prepared any learning experience" (p. 48). These two quotes encapsulate the purpose behind this book. The first quote places teaching and learning as almost an afterthought that must somehow flow automatically from the store of knowledge that has been acquired during doctoral work. The second quote illustrates that, given the opportunity and support to do so, faculty will be energized to develop vibrant learning experiences where both they and their students are mutually engaged in constructing new understandings and discovering new insights in their disciplines.

It should also be noted that at the higher education level, teaching is sometimes referred to as andragogy as opposed to pedagogy for Pre-12 students. Adult learners in higher education value attributes of learning differently than younger learners. As Evans (2015) points out:

> While important, grades are not always the prime focus of adult learners. Intellectual discourse, engagement with the material and other students, sharing of

experiences, relating the lesson to real-world examples, and recognizing adult learners' professional backgrounds all help to keep the adult learner engaged. (p. 19)

As we consider the similarities that exist among all organizations due to the need to operate amidst social, economic, and political influences, the unique mission of higher education is demarcated from most other organizations in a fundamental way. The very nature of higher education, especially the unfettered pursuit of individual scholarly inquiry within the various academic disciplines, serves to fragment the overall higher education structure and results in unique impediments to change, especially at it pertains to professional development. Meanwhile, looming across the entire horizon in higher education is the sometimes underappreciated challenge of meeting the needs of our adult learners.

4.5. IMPEDIMENTS TO CHANGE IN HIGHER EDUCATION

While higher education takes great pride in discovering new knowledge and its applications, neither it nor its practitioners are immune to a natural aversion to change! The uncertainty caused by changes in leadership, policies, and technology typically results in resistance to change among both staff and faculty. The rhetorical question posed by Senge (1990), "who could resist the benefits of personal mastery?" (p. 135), has special significance for higher education, particularly when the issue is professional development.

Perhaps the most visible barrier to change in higher education is when change is perceived as a threat to academic freedom. As Tierney (2008) noted, academic disciplines that give *shape* to life within higher education and serve as the lens through which faculty often view proposed changes. Cole (2009) cites political threats to academic freedom caused by governmental responses to war and more recently to terrorism. He also indicates that even though systematic empirical studies have not established a definite causal connection between the value and frequency of new discoveries and academic freedom, he nevertheless argues that if we curtail academic freedom "we threaten the ability of universities to make great discoveries, and we potentially sacrifice the fruits of both the transmission of knowledge and the creation of new knowledge – knowledge on which our society greatly depends" (p. 347).

While it is the creation of knowledge that speaks most directly to research and scholarship, the transmission of knowledge is most easily seen in the classroom. Teaching practice underlies this transmission and is the primary concern here. Because there is a perceived connection between the tenets of what is considered quality scholarship and teaching practice, resistance to change will likely occur when attempting to establish Centers for Teaching Excellence that propose only one particular way to improve teaching skills and competencies in the higher education classroom.

Another sensitive area that we believe manifests itself as resistance to change is an unwillingness of faculty to expose any shortcomings they may have in terms of teaching and classroom effectiveness. It is certainly understandable that faculty would not want to appear lacking in areas where they are expected to be experts. Self-esteem can be a fragile commodity causing them to *circle the wagons*!

Burgan (2006) when discussing both the *reformers of pedagogy* and the *reformers of the curriculum* classify the former group as constructivists and the latter as classicists. She continues by saying that, while she sympathizes with both points of view, "each can state its position in such extreme ways, and so simplistically, that classroom teachers are likely to respond to either with skepticism" (p. 25). Perhaps it is skepticism as much as perceived threats to self-esteem that can result in faculty resisting efforts to establish Centers for Teaching Excellence and therefore both of these impediments must be taken into account when embarking on a change effort that can be perceived as either threatening or ephemeral, or both.

Burgan also argues that the reward system must include a "sponsorship of teaching" (p. 25) for teaching reform efforts to be successful. This admonition not only illuminates an impediment to change but goes further by pointing out that faculty need to see clearly how the proposed reform connects to the promotion and tenure structure and that their support of and active participation in the proposed reform will lead to both professional and personal growth.

The impact of threats to academic freedom and self-esteem, skepticism toward reform efforts, and the need to incentivize these reforms by linking them to the existing reward system represent powerful influences that have been identified in the literature and that must be considered when seeking to establish Centers for Teaching Excellence.

4.6 TECHNOLOGY

The role of technology from the perspective of organizations has many similarities to higher education. Senge (2006) illustrates the need for organizations to become *learning organizations*. This admonition applies equally to colleges and universities as well. The importance of technology to higher education's core mission of teaching and learning cannot be overstated. The Vygotskian emphasis on the role of cultural tools in learning finds concrete applications in classrooms and laboratories throughout academe. A cursory walk through of any college library or classroom will find students on their laptops and professors projecting their presentations using an endless variety of hardware and software. The only thing certain is that change is the only constant when it comes to technology in higher education.

As with most other innovations, there is not universal agreement as to the benefits and drawbacks of technology. While there is no denying that technology in all its myriad forms is here to stay and will continue to mutate, most faculty (and administrators) have at some time questioned the true value of technology for teaching and learning.

Luke (2010) raises some legitimate questions regarding the nature and impact of both interdisciplinary and digital initiatives on college campuses. He cautions that "digitalization relies upon a very conventional modernization narrative that poses it as an always progressive force breaking apart old corrupt traditions. Still, this ideological conceit is no guarantee that digitalization automatically brings forth a better, bolder, bigger way of doing scholarly activity" (p. 73). While we all use and appreciate the benefits of technology, as scholars we also have the responsibility to examine and question each application of technology within our sphere of influence. Although the Bio-ecological Model does not specifically identify technology, we can easily think of the myriad roles and significant impacts of technology within every circular component of this system as we go about our daily work in higher education.

The IRM was developed to help faculty improve their teaching effectiveness by providing a confidential way to self-assess and integrate pedagogy and technology into a personal professional development plan. As faculty improve their instructional practice, technology poses special problems. Fortunately, we have the IRM to predict and promote acceptance along with a number of motivational and cognitive theories.

As stated earlier, faculty are intrinsically motivated to learn and excel in both teaching and scholarship (Stipek, 2002). Other theories of technology acceptance examine the intention to use technology as well as the degree of actual use (Lasumer & Eckhardt, 2012). The technology acceptance model offers yet another way to understand technology acceptance based on the assumption that faculty will accept technology if they perceive that it is actually useful to the teaching process and they possess the required knowledge and skills to use it effectively (Turner et al., 2010). The IRM was developed with these considerations in mind. But its success ultimately depends on its acceptance not only by faculty but also by the leadership in higher education and their willingness to invest in Centers for Teaching Excellence that use the IRM as a professional development tool.

4.7. GENERATIONAL LABELS

The readiness to use technology was highlighted in the previous chapter. Differences among three recognized generations – Baby Boomers (1946–1965), Gen Xers (1966–1979), and Millennials (1980 and later) – were considered. The generations may help explain resistance to change when it comes to the integration of technology into higher education. Expect a degree of variation within each of these groups.

From a student perspective, today's undergraduates are primarily Millennials (Figure 4.1). However, it may be the case that new categories of students will emerge based on new demographic factors including even more sophisticated technology or perhaps the impact of terrorism. Nonetheless, for now because undergraduate students are *digital natives*, the vast majority have grown up using technology in virtually every aspect of their lives headed by the ubiquitous smart phone with all of its apps and impact on communications and interpersonal relationships. It is to be expected that these students are ready, willing, and able to continue to learn and utilize new instructional technologies in higher education.

Graduate students, too, are currently more diverse in terms of their generational category, expectations, and readiness to use instructional technologies (Figure 4.2). Variations within categories are to be expected with graduate students as well; awareness of this diversity may be helpful to faculty as they plan and develop their courses.

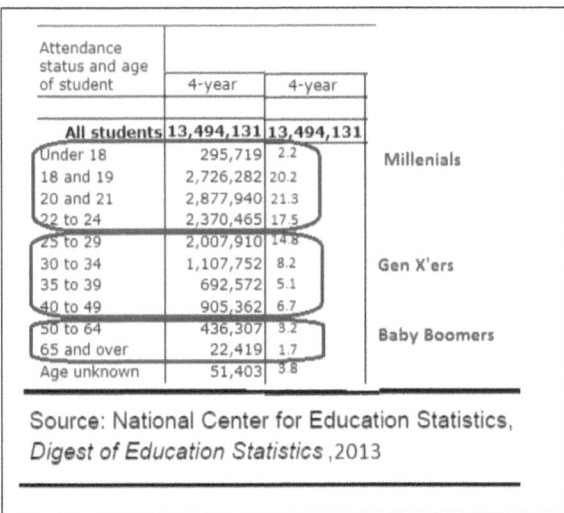

Figure 4.1 Undergraduate Enrollment by Age. *Source*: Author-developed for this book.

Graduate Enrollment by Age, Fall 2007

	Fall 2007		
	Number	**%**	
All Students	2,293,593	100%	
Under 18	215	0%	
18 and 19	931	0%	Post-Millenials
20 and 21	18,751	1%	
22 to 24	401,589	18%	
25 to 29	701,462	31%	
30 to 34	390,025	17%	Millenials
35 to 39	258,480	11%	
40 to 49	318,074	14%	Gen X'ers
50 to 64	175,838	8%	
65 and over	6,483	0%	Baby Boomers
Age unknown	21,745	1%	
29 and under	1,122,948	49%	
30 to 39	648,505	28%	
40 and over	500,395	22%	

Source: National Center for Education Statistics, *Digest of Education Statistics*, 2008

Figure 4.2. Graduate Enrollment by Age. *Source:* Author-developed for this book.

Similarly, faculty are also diverse in terms of their generational identities (Figure 4.3.). This mixture of generations with their associated differences in experiences and cultural expectations presents yet another potential complexity regarding impediments to change.

A Center for Teaching Excellence, fueled by the IRM model, attempts to influence pedagogical practice of faculty as they develop over a lifelong academic career. It is exactly these concerns that any successful change effort in higher education faculty development must recognize and try to incorporate if there is to be any reasonable chance of success.

4.8. MOVING FORWARD

The previous section admonished the reader that successful change efforts in higher education must recognize that faculty are highly educated professionals who are primarily self-directed. Any suggested innovations must be perceived as relevant, nonthreatening, and conducive to achieving their goals for professional growth – exactly the right starting point in order to overcome

Selected characteristic	Number (thousands)
Full-time faculty and instructional staff	
Number (in thousands)	681.8 (0.05)
Percentage distribution	
Age	
Under 35	59.1 (1.77) — Millenials
35 to 44	169.8 (2.78)
45 to 54	219.7 (3.28) — Gen X'ers
55 to 64	190.0 (3.10)
65 to 69	31.8 (1.43)
70 or older	11.5 (0.67) — Baby Boomers

Source: National Center for Education Statistics, *Digest of Education Statistics*, 2013

Figure 4.3. Faculty by Age. *Source*: Author-developed for this book.

resistance to constructing centers for teaching excellence. Start with the recognition that the core mission of higher education is teaching and scholarly pursuits. Then build an organizational structure that supports each faculty member's efforts to grow in both of these areas.

The IRM was developed as a personal tool to evaluate faculty strengths and weaknesses. Used correctly, it can play a valuable role in their development. As described in both this and the previous chapter, individuality is inextricably connected with both social influences and cultural surroundings. And so, we came to recognize fairly early on that while the IRM must come to be perceived as relevant and useful to individual faculty member, the achievement of goals depends not solely on individual efforts but also the support and encouragement of an organization informed by the factors related to successful implementation.

We therefore suggest that those responsible for constructing and administering any program related to faculty development think of the relationship between faculty and the organizational structure designed to support individual faculty efforts as being flexibly coupled rather than tightly or loosely coupled. Higher education is unlike other organizations found in the business or military world. The culture in higher education is simply not consistent with the concept of tight coupling.

Higher education functions better when its mindset views individuals as the center of change and that such change is a process and not an event (Hall & Hord, 1987). In other words, what is required is an approach that recognizes that over-rationalization is inconsistent with the realities found in higher education. Excellence in teaching, learning, and scholarship actually comes about when organizational initiatives seeking to facilitate growth are based on this understanding.

REFERENCES

Bain, K. (2004). *What the best college teachers do.* Cambridge, MA: Harvard University Press.

Baldridge, J.V. (1983). Organizational characteristics of colleges and universities. In J. V. Baldridge & T. Deal (Eds.), *The dynamics of organizational change in education* (pp. 38–59). Berkeley, CA: McCutchan Publishing Corporation.

Burgan, M. (2006). *What ever happened to the faculty?* Baltimore, MD: The John Hopkins University Press.

Cole, J.R. (2009). *The great American university: Its rise to preeminence, its indispensable national role, why it must be protected.* New York, NY: Public Affairs.

Evans, T. (2015). Engaging the adult learner. In L. Tomei (Ed.), *Teaching in higher education: Becoming college faculty* (pp. 17–22). Pittsburgh, PA: RMU University Press.

Gage, N. L. (1989). The paradigm wars and their aftermath: A "historical" sketch of research on teaching since 1989. *Educational Researcher, 18*(7), 4–10.

Hall, G. E., & Hord, S. M. (1987). *Change in schools: Facilitating the process.* Albany, NY: State University of New York Press.

Laumer, S., & Eckhardt, A. (2012). Why do people reject technologies: a review of user resistance theories. *Information systems theory* (pp. 63–86). New York, NY: Springer.

Luke, T. W. (2010). What is information? The neoliberal turn, digitalization, and interdisciplinarity. In S. J. Rosow and T. Kriger (Eds.), *Transforming higher education* (pp. 65–80). Lanham, MD: Lexington Books.

Porter, M. E. (1980). *Competitive strategy: Techniques for analyzing industries and competitors.* New York, NY: Free Press.

Senge, P. M. (1990). *The fifth discipline. The art and practice of the learning organization.* New York, NY: Currency Doubleday.

Senge, P. M. (2006). *The fifth discipline. The art and practice of the learning organization.* New York, NY: Currency Doubleday.

Stipek, D. J. (2002). Motivation to learn. *Integrating theory and practice* (4th ed.). Boston, MA: Allyn & Bacon.

Tierney, W. G. (2008). *The impact of culture on organizational decision making: Theory and practice in higher education.* Sterling, VA: Stylus

Turner, M., Kitchenham, B., Brereton, P., Charters, S., & Budgen, D. (2010). Does the technology acceptance model predict actual use? *Information and Software Technology, 52*, 463–479.

Weick, K. (1983). Educational organizations as loosely coupled systems. In J. V. Baldridge & T. Deal (Eds.), *The dynamics of organizational change in education* (pp. 15–37). Berkeley, CA: McCutchan Publishing Corporation.

Part III

THE FOUNDATIONAL CONCEPTS OF THE IRM

Part Three offers the readers the foundational concepts of the Integrated Readiness Matrix (IRM). Chapter 5 explores the IRM as a tool for advancing critical higher education faculty skills and competencies along the two dimensions of pedagogy and technology.

Chapter 6 examines pedagogical skills and competencies and suggests specific skills and competencies. Content knowledge, skills acquisition, and teaching are matched with pedagogy. Hardware, software, skills acquisition, and learning and teaching are tied to technology. Some 70 teaching episodes are recommended for each of the five quadrants of the IRM. Use these episodes to prepare your faculty and advance them from appreciative to master integrator.

The process of plotting an initial location on the X–Y grid is a key objective of this text. Faculty will learn how to assess where they are and where they need to improve with respect to pedagogy and technology. The steps provided in chapter 7 lead them toward the goal of becoming a Master Integrator. The establishment of a professional development program is possible by drawing on many resources recommended in this text.

Chapter 5

Forming the Dimensions of the Integrated Readiness Matrix

5.1. INTRODUCTION

This chapter explores the Integrated Readiness Matrix (IRM) as a tool for advancing critical higher education faculty skills and competencies along the two dimensions of pedagogy and technology.

Integrating Pedagogy and Technology: Improving Teaching and Learning in Higher Education (Bernauer & Tomei, 2015) provided a more exhaustive review of the IRM. We offer here a brief recap of how the five primary schools of educational psychology (behaviorism, cognitivism, humanism, constructivism, and connectivism) establish the theoretical foundation for the skills and competencies required of higher education classroom faculty. Next, chapter 6 will move quickly into a discussion of those skills and competencies and chapter 7 will present the practical expression of the IRM and the tools to locate yourself on the X–Y dimensions of the IRM.

5.2. THE IRM: GROUNDED IN MANAGEMENT THEORY

The Managerial Grid by Robert Blake and Jane Mouton (1964) provides the underlying construct for the IRM across two different behavioral dimensions. Blake and Mouton offer the management scholar an examination of concern for people versus concern for production.

Early critics and proponents of the Managerial Grid including Keys (1977), Bernardin and Alvares (1976), Mckee (2005), and Bryman (2007) argue that the original nine-by-nine matrix was too granular, overstating distinguishing quadrant characteristics of the grid. Further literature supporting the grid ultimately produced five easily identifiable leadership styles.

Although written with a business focus in mind, researchers have successfully applied the five styles to many other leadership applications, for example, higher education. One such study, *Developing a Leadership Perspective in the Classroom* (Barbuto, 2000), presented a model that integrated leadership theory and student development. The model has helped faculty make strategic instructional choices rather than relying on traditionally accepted teaching styles. Its major contribution is the use of leadership theory to identify and develop teaching styles based on the developmental and motivational needs of students.

Another study, *Learner-Centered Instruction (LCI)* versus *Teacher-Centered Instruction (TCI): A Classroom Management Perspective* (Minter, 2011) employed the Managerial Grid as a model to encourage teacher education to incorporate management and leadership training with an emphasis on students. Its main contention was that classroom instructors are managers and leaders as well as teachers. Therefore, management concepts should apply to the classroom environment.

These studies provide a perspective of the Managerial Grid (Figure 5.1.) with respect to higher education and college faculty (with apologies to Blake & Mouton).

Typical of the *Novice Educator*, faculty in this quadrant of the grid are still learning the demands of their classroom or administrative positions. They must be supported and mentored to create efficient and effective teaching and learning environments.

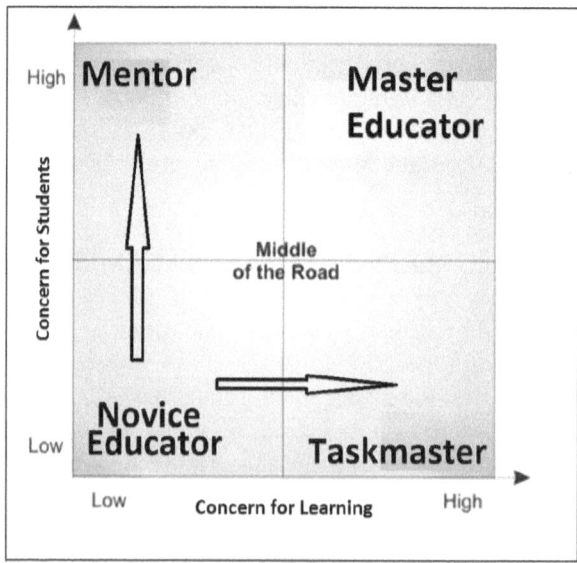

Figure 5.1 Blake-Mouton Managerial Grid (a higher education outlook). *Source*: Author-developed for this book.

From a standing start, educators in our example move in one of two directions: either a concern for students or a concern for learning – often to the exclusion of the other, at least initially. In that respect, they are similar to their business and management counterparts. Let's continue examining the other quadrants.

Often, apprentice faculty are called on to serve as *Mentors* – advisors and counselors for students in their academic disciplines. Mentors evidence the greatest concern for students making the (sometimes incorrect) assumption that happy students will work hard. Such an exclusive concern for individual needs and feelings often negatively impacts learning. Such faculty find it difficult to assign grades, much less an inferior grade, especially if the student seemingly worked hard during the term. As a result, the relationship here in this quadrant is characterized as casual, friendly, advisory, but not very task-oriented.

While some faculty embrace the role of advisor and mentor, others take a more hard-line approach to the classroom. The *Taskmaster* shows less regard for a student's personal situation, for example, family, work-related responsibilities, perhaps even individual (and disparate) learning styles. Their job is to teach; the student's responsibility is to learn.

Educators functioning at the *Middle-of-the-road* level settle for average performance from their students and seldom push the boundaries of learning beyond the classroom.

The upper-right quadrant of the grid is for the *Master Educator* in the same manner as it was the target goal for Blake and Mouton's top managers. Characteristically, high concern for learning is matched with a high concern for the learner. Experienced teachers feel empowered, equally and strongly committed to both their students and the academic discipline they represent. They respect a classroom atmosphere that results in high student satisfaction and well-documented learning outcomes.

5.3. CONVERTING THE MANAGERIAL GRID TO THE IRM

The transformation of the business-oriented Managerial Grid to the IRM calls for substituting the dimensions of the X–Y axes with education-related interests. To begin, the concern for people dimension of the Y-axis is converted into the pedagogical dimension; then, the concern for production becomes the technological dimension of the IRM.

- *The Pedagogical Dimension (Y-Axis)*. The IRM incorporates Bloom's Taxonomy as well as concepts borrowed from the schools of educational psychology discussed in chapter 1.

- *The Technological Dimension (X-Axis).* The Taxonomy for the Technology Domain offered in chapter 2 serves as the pivotal focus for the technological X-axis of the IRM.

Both the Y-axis (pedagogy) and the X-axis (technology) suggest a new and innovative perspective of teaching and learning to achieve outcomes for higher education (Figure 5.2). Integrating Bloom's revised taxonomy and Tomei's taxonomy for the technology domain results in a corresponding set of quadrants similar to Blake and Mouton's Managerial Grid.

The *Apprentice Integrator* utilizes lower order thinking skills on the pedagogical level – those most closely associated with remembering, understanding, and applying. In a similar vein, the apprentice uses the lower levels of literacy, communications, and decision-making in the application of technological tools for teaching. Faculty at the college and university level are characteristically hired because of their discipline-specific track record; that is, they are recognized for their mastery as an engineer or their scholarly achievements in writing or research. Most were provided little to no training in the areas of classroom pedagogy or instructional technology. As a result,

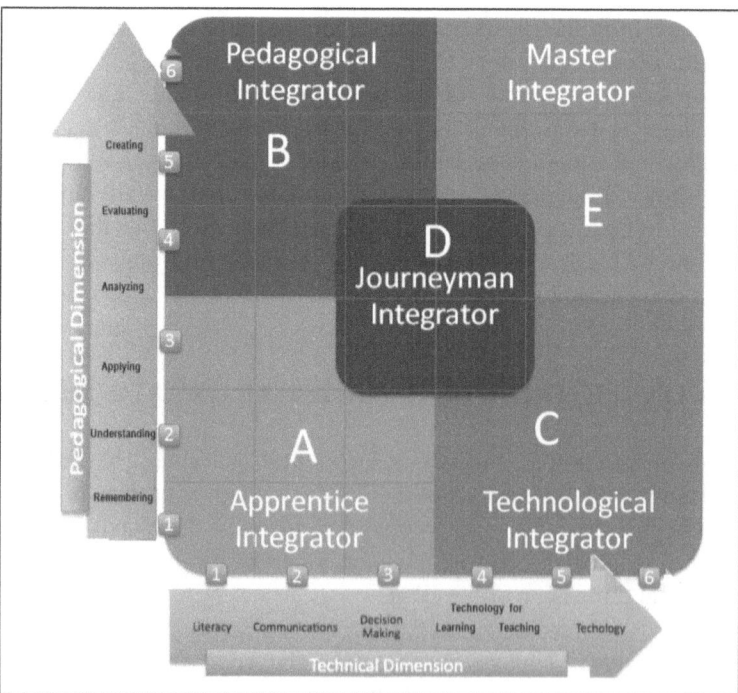

Figure 5.2 **The Integrated Readiness Matrix.** *Source*: Author-developed for this book.

new higher education faculty tend to spend an inordinate amount of time in the lower levels of both Bloom's Taxonomy (Garavalia, Hummel, Wiley, & Huitt, 1999) and the Technology Taxonomy (Tomei, 2005).

The *Pedagogical Integrator* is most likely a gifted teacher who understands the importance of careful instructional design and the application of sound teaching principles. Higher order thinking skills are to be found in his or her classroom (traditional or online). Analyzing, evaluating, and creating are the norms with objectives that challenge the learner to generate new ideas, criticize and judge, and reflect on subject matter. Educators in this quadrant lack affection if not an affinity for educational technology. They do not appreciate the grip that technology has on the twenty-first-century students.

If they are older faculty, technology may intimidate. For younger faculty, the veil of incompetence may be frightening. For others, technology may not impress as does a well-practiced lecture. Instructors who adopt this attitude likely have a long track record of successful teaching and find it counterproductive to *clutter* their delivery with technology. Regardless, the Pedagogical Integrator can be very difficult to win over (the term *curmudgeon* comes to mind) since they believe what they have done in the past will continue to bear fruit given sufficiently motivated students.

The *Technological Integrator* would marry technology with instruction better than most, creating multimedia presentations that astonish the learner and amaze the neophyte technologist. The use of technology is pervasive in their teaching and at times may prove overwhelming to their students. Truth be told, many in this quadrant dazzle their students with technology skills intended to deflect attention away from their lack of teaching skills or mastery of the content. Successful at first, students quickly see through the veil and often avoid such faculty when registering for next semester's courses.

The *Journeyman Integrator* is most common in higher education; the majority of faculty would place themselves in this quadrant. Some Journeymen embrace new technologies; others feel no obligation whatsoever to integrate the latest technology simply because every student in class happens to own an iPhone, a PDA, or a Facebook account.

Master Integrators are the epitome of classroom instructors. They understand the effective use of varied instructional strategies and possess a solid understanding of how taxonomies impact teaching, learning, student motivation, and learning outcomes. Such instructors tend to be self-motivated, equally eager to adopt new pedagogies, and implement the latest technologies. They are early adopters if they believe there are benefits to their students.

Master Integrators challenge learners by offering instruction at the highest levels of the pedagogical and technological domains. They extend classroom instruction beyond the basics and are not threatened when students evidence a higher degree of skill in either domain – especially technology. Such college and university instructors typically create learning assessments that offer students not only the opportunity to demonstrate mastery of the content through traditional means but also a chance to synthesize what they know into new knowledge.

5.3. CONCLUSION

Chapter 5 establishes the parameters of the IRM and its foundation of pedagogy and technology. Bloom's Taxonomy defines the Y-axis as it moves pedagogical skills from remembering to creating. Tomei's Taxonomy advances technological skills from literacy to tech-ology.

Now that we have the quadrants established, we will explore specific skills and competencies that college and university faculty should master as they move from the lower left of the matrix to the upper-right corner. Suffice it say at this point that personal experience and research suggest that too much teaching occurs at the lower levels of both taxonomies, even in colleges and universities.

REFERENCES

Barbuto Jr. J. (2000). Developing a Leadership Perspective in the Classroom, University of Nebraska – Lincoln, 2000.

Bernardin John H and Alvares Kenneth M. (1976). The Managerial Grid as a Conflict.

Bernauer, James A. and Tomei, Lawrence A. (2015). Integrating Pedagogy and Technology: Improving Teaching and Learning in Higher Education.

Blake Robert R and Mouton S. Jane (1964) The Managerial Grid, Houston Gulf Publishing.

Bryman, A. (2007). Effective leadership in higher education: A literature review. *Studies in Higher Education, 32*(6), 693–710.

Eisenmann, L. (2004). Integrating disciplinary perspectives into higher education research; The example of history. *The Journal of Higher Education, 75*(1), 7–22.

Garavalia, L., Hummel, J., Wiley, L., & Huitt, W. (1999). Constructing the course syllabus: Faculty and student perceptions of important syllabus components. *Journal of Excellence in College Teaching, 10*(1), 5–22. Available online at http://www.edpsycinteractive.org/papers/cons_course_syll.doc

Keys E. Bernard (1977) Management of Learning Grid for Managerial Development, *The Academy of Management Review, 2*(2), 289–292.

Mckee Rachel (2005). The Grid Difference: A Historical Perspective of Grid.

Minter, Mary Kennedy (2011). Learner-Centered Instruction (LCI) vs. Teacher-Centered Instruction (TCI): A Classroom Management Perspective, *American Journal of Business Education*, 4(5), 55–62.

Northouse, P. G. (2013). Leadership: Theory and Practice (6th ed.). Thousand Oaks, CA, SAGE Publications, Inc.

Tomei, Lawrence A. *Taxonomy for the Technology Domain: A Classification of Educational Objectives for the Technology Domain*, Idea Group Publishers, Inc. 2005.

Wordpress, 2014. Risk Profile Improvement. http://riskmanagement365.wordpress.com /2012/12/22/ what-is-blake-moutons-managerial-grid/blake-and-mouton-leadership-grid/.

Chapter 6

The Skills and Competencies of the Integrated Readiness Matrix

6.1. INTRODUCTION

Too often efforts at improving how we teach are sidetracked by predictable impediments: competing time demands, institutional budget limitations, prevailing ideological misunderstandings, lack of faculty accountability for delivering engaging instruction, commitments to research and scholarly inquiry, personal obligations, and others. These examples can limit professional development – during one particular semester or over an entire career in higher education.

This chapter will examine pedagogical skills and competencies that focus on content knowledge, skills acquisition, and teaching as well as technological skills and competencies including hardware, software, skills acquisition, and learning and teaching with technology.

It offers the readers a comprehensive, detailed look at nearly 70 teaching episodes for consideration in each of the five quadrants of the Integrated Readiness Matrix (IRM; Figure 6.1.) to move faculty from appreciative to master integrator.

Approximately 300 distinct skills and competencies are categorized into one of the five quadrants of the IRM.

6.2. SKILLS AND COMPETENCIES OF THE IRM

Each skill/competency is identified with a specific pedagogical and/or technological focus. Pedagogical skills are associated with (C)ontent knowledge, (SA) Skills Acquisition, and (T)eaching. Technological opportunities address (H)ardware, (S)oftware, (SA) Skills Acquisition, (L)earning with technology, and (T)eaching with technology.

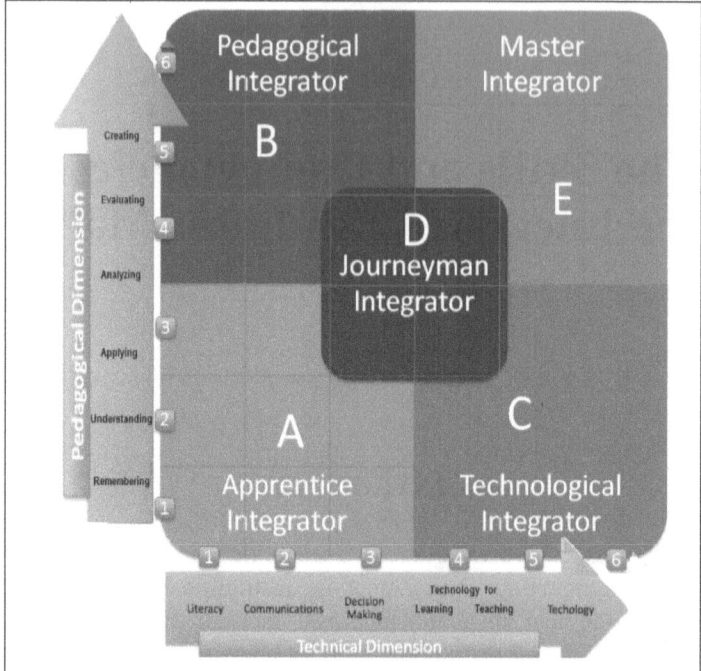

Figure 6.1 The Integrated Readiness Matrix. *Source*: Author-developed for this book.

Appendix D offers expanded activity descriptions and learning outcomes for each of the recommended teaching episodes. Readers can dig down into a description of each activity and its specific learning outcomes. Use this additional information to build your own workshops, seminars, roundtables, colloquiums, or training sessions for your faculty.

6.2.1. Apprentice Integrator (Appendix D, A.1–A.11)

At the *Apprentice Integrator* stage, a faculty member is taking off the training wheels. Faculty in this quadrant offer students a baseline challenge; deliver rote names, dates, and events; and provide a sequenced approach to the content they expect students to master. Technology is employed cautiously, if at all. It might be visible in the classroom, but serves primarily a tangential role in lectures or classroom discussions.

Eleven teaching episodes (Figure 6.2.) are suggested for your consideration and most of those specifically relate to content knowledge and teaching competence. Use the teaching episodes shown with an (A)pprentice prefix in Appendix D to initiate a program to prepare new faculty in the skills and competencies of the Apprentice Integrator.

The Skills and Competencies of the Integrated Readiness Matrix

	Apprentice Integrator								
		Pedagogy			Technology				
	Skill/Competency	P-C	P-SA	P-T	T-H	T-S	T-SA	T-L	T-T
A.1	The Pillars of Education			P-T					
A.2	Learning Theories -- A Primer Exercise	P-C		P-T					
A.3	First Year College Students Demographics			P-T					
A.4	College Student Subpopulations			P-T					
A.5	Historical Perspectives of Higher Education	P-C		P-T					
A.6	Model for Differentiating Teaching and Learning			P-T					
A.7	Hierarchy of Human Needs	P-C							
A.8	Taxonomy for the Technology Domain							T-L	T-T
A.9	Classroom Diversity	P-C							
A.10	Servant Leadership	P-C							
A.11	Academic Problems and Mental Health Challenges			P-T					

See Appendix A for Skills/Competencies and Learning Outcomes

P-C	Pedagogy - Content knowledge
P-SA	Pedagogy - Skills Acquisition
P-T	Pedagogy - Teaching competence
T-H	Technology - Hardware
T-S	Technology - Software
T-SA	Technology - Skills Acquisition
T-L	Technology - Learning
T-T	Technology - Teaching

Figure 6.2 The Skills and Competencies of the Apprentice Integrator. *Source*: Author-developed for this book.

6.2.2. Pedagogical Integrator (Appendix D, P.1–P.15)

The *Pedagogical Integrator* might demand analysis, synthesis, evaluation, or the creation of original work from the students. But the challenge to think critically may not be matched with a breadth of technological tools. In fact, the greatest demonstration of technology might come outside the classroom as the instructor communicates via e-mail with students or uses decision-making software to simulate a real-world learning outcome.

We offer 15 teaching episodes (Figure 6.3.) to bring faculty up to speed with respect to pedagogy. Keep in mind that most higher education faculty (unless they are graduates from a school of education) may not been exposed to pedagogy-based courses or formal teacher preparation programs. These episodes focus primarily on acquiring teaching skills and building instructor competence. Use the teaching episodes shown with a (P)edagogical prefix in Appendix D to design a program for faculty in the skills and competencies of the pedagogical integrator.

6.2.3. Technological Integrator (Appendix D, T.1–T.10)

Faculty who find themselves in this quadrant of the IRM might dazzle students with their wizardry of technology but may not deliver an equally

Pedagogical Integrator		Pedagogy			Technology				
	Skill/Competency	P-C	P-SA	P-T	T-H	T-S	T-SA	T-L	T-T
P.1	Constructivism	P-C	P-SA	P-T					
P.2	Connectivism	P-C	P-SA	P-T				T-L	
P.3	Teaching Behaviorally			P-T					
P.4	Classical and Operant Conditioning			P-T					
P.5	Reinforcement Schedules			P-T					
P.6	Social Learning Theories			P-T					
P.7	Programmed Instruction			P-T				T-L	T-T
P.8	Behavioral Learning Objectives			P-T					
P.9	Zone of Proximal Development	P-C	P-SA	P-T					
P.10	Stages of Cognitive Development			P-T					
P.11	Cooperative Learning Theories	P-C	P-SA	P-T					
P.12	Individual Constructivism	P-C	P-SA	P-T					
P.13	Social Constructivism	P-C	P-SA						
P.14	Assessment of Teaching and Learning			P-T					
P.15	Diversity of Learning Strategies			P-T					

See Appendix A for Skills/Competencies and Learning Outcomes

P-C   Pedagogy - Content knowledge
P-SA   Pedagogy - Skills Acquisition
P-T   Pedagogy - Teaching competence
T-H   Technology - Hardware
T-S   Technology - Software
T-SA   Technology - Skills Acquisition
T-L   Technology - Learning
T-T   Technology - Teaching

Figure 6.3 The Skills and Competencies of the Pedagogical Integrator. *Source*: Author-developed for this book.

powerful pedagogical lesson. Often, students find themselves unclear about how a piece of technology is relevant to the learning at hand. Imagine, for example, populating a spreadsheet with various data, but not being able to explain what those cells or individual datum mean and why they are necessary to know.

Ten teaching episodes (Figure 6.4.) address the general technological underpinnings of faculty. Each institution will assuredly be adding its own unique competencies based on its choice of hardware, software, and network packages. Notice that the skills and competencies detailed in Figure 6.4. are nearly evenly split between technology and pedagogy. To do otherwise would sever an important linkage between teaching and technology; they must work in harmony to produce an effective lesson. Faculty workshops and seminars highlighting skills acquisition remain important; however, even more significant is an understanding that technology for teaching and learning must move faculty through the technology quadrant toward journeyman and master. Use the episodes shown with a (T)echnological prefix in Appendix D to design a program for faculty that meld teaching, learning, and technology into a seamless instructional strategy for the classroom.

The Skills and Competencies of the Integrated Readiness Matrix 63

Technological Integrator

	Skill/Competency	Pedagogy			Technology				
		P-C	P-SA	P-T	T-H	T-S	T-SA	T-L	T-T
T.1	Open Education Resources					T-S	T-SA	T-L	
T.2	Online Teaching and Learning			P-T				T-L	T-T
T.3	Impact of Online Teaching on Faculty Load			P-T					T-T
T.4	Massive Open Online Courses (MOOCs)			P-T				T-L	T-T
T.5	Faculty Attitudes Toward Technology			P-T	T-H	T-S	T-SA	T-L	T-T
T.6	Relating Technology to Theories of Learning	P-C						T-L	T-T
T.7	Educational Software	P-C	P-SA	P-T		T-S			
T.8	Communications, Networks, and the Internet				T-H	T-S	T-SA	T-L	T-T
T.9	Technology Standards for Teaching	P-C	P-SA	P-T			T-SA		
T.10	Internet Exploration and Harvesting			P-T				T-L	

See Appendix C for Skills/Competencies and Learning Outcomes

P-C	Pedagogy - Content knowledge
P-SA	Pedagogy - Skills Acquisition
P-T	Pedagogy - Teaching competence
T-H	Technology - Hardware
T-S	Technology - Software
T-SA	Technology - Skills Acquisition
T-L	Technology - Learning
T-T	Technology - Teaching

Figure 6.4 The Skills and Competencies of the Technological Integrator. *Source:* Author-developed for this book.

6.2.4. Journeyman Integrator (Appendix C, J.1–J.17)

Journeyman Integrators are most likely to be respected by their colleagues and students. By all accounts, they challenge their students through interesting and relevant assignments and stimulate learning through technological applications appropriate for the content.

Most teaching episodes (Figure 6.5.) occur in the mid-level quadrant of the matrix spilling over the boundaries of the other four quadrants. Most educators spend the majority of their career as journeymen. Some 17 teaching episodes are offered, running the gamut from professional writing to creating text, visual, and web-based instructional materials. Use the teaching episodes shown with a (J)ourneyman prefix in Appendix D to put together a comprehensive, professional development program for the lifelong learner/educator seeking currency with the latest theories and technologies and continuous improvement of his or her classroom delivery.

6.2.5. Master Integrator (Appendix D, M.1–M.11)

Faculty who migrate to the *Master Integrator* level are at the pinnacle of their higher education careers. Not only do they inspire their students (and perhaps

	Journeyman Integrator								
		Pedagogy			Technology				
	Skill/Competency	P-C	P-SA	P-T	T-H	T-S	T-SA	T-L	T-T
J.1	Effective Professional Writing		P-SA	P-T					T-T
J.2	Guide to a Successful Book Proposal		P-SA						T-T
J.3	Discovery and Reception Learning		P-SA	P-T					
J.4	Information Processing Model		P-SA	P-T					
J.5	Andragogy: the Study of Adult Learning Styles	P-C		P-T				T-L	
J.6	Psychosocial Development	P-C		P-T					
J.7	Ethics in the Classroom	P-C	P-SA						
J.8	ISD Models	P-C	P-SA	P-T					
J.9	Introduction to Instructional System Design	P-C	P-SA	P-T					
J.10	Learning Transfer Model	P-C	P-SA	P-T					
J.11	The Teacher/Scholar Model	P-C	P-SA	P-T					
J.12	Assessing Technology and Evaluating Student Learning		P-SA	P-T				T-L	X
J.13	Integration of Technology-rich Resources			P-T			T-SA	T-L	T-T
J.14	Creating Text-Based Student Materials			P-T			T-SA	T-L	T-T
J.15	Creating Visual-Based Classroom Presentations			P-T			T-SA	T-L	T-T
J.16	Creating Web-Based Classroom Presentations			P-T			T-SA	T-L	T-T
J.17	Andragogy and Technology: Integrating Adult Learning			P-T			T-SA	T-L	T-T

See Appendix D for Skills/Competencies and Learning Outcomes

P-C   Pedagogy - Content knowledge
P-SA   Pedagogy - Skills Acquisition
P-T   Pedagogy - Teaching competence
T-H   Technology - Hardware
T-S   Technology - Software
T-SA   Technology - Skills Acquisition
T-L   Technology - Learning
T-T   Technology - Teaching

Figure 6.5 **The Skills and Competencies of the Journeyman Integrator.** *Source*: Author-developed for this book.

their faculty colleagues) with their content knowledge and pedagogical application, but they are at the top of their game with respect to their technological skills. At this level, faculty might explain how plagiarism software works and demonstrate it to the students while engaging in dialogue with the creators of that software about its positive attributes and shortcomings.

Teaching episodes (Figure 6.6.) here are more wide-ranging in their scope and more restrictive in their audience. Faculty who placed themselves in the uppermost quadrant are invited to these workshops to address the highest level of the pedagogical and technology taxonomies. Use the teaching episodes shown with an (M)aster prefix to offer a limited number of targeted episodes throughout the academic year.

6.3. SUMMARY

The IRM contains five quadrants: (A)*pprentice Integrator* suggests that the educator is scratching the surface of his or her capabilities as an educator in the classroom in both pedagogy and technology. (P)*edagogical Integrator*

The Skills and Competencies of the Integrated Readiness Matrix

	Master Integrator	Pedagogy			Technology				
	Skill/Competency	P-C	P-SA	P-T	T-H	T-S	T-SA	T-L	T-T
M.1	Interprofessional Learning	P-C	P-SA	P-T					
M.2	Multiple Intelligences	P-C	P-SA	P-T				T-L	
M.3	Integrated Readiness Matrix			P-T				T-L	T-T
M.4	Personal Learning Networks		P-SA	P-T					T-T
M.5	Differentiated Instruction		P-SA	P-T					
M.6	Flipped Learning		P-SA	P-T					
M.7	Blended Learning		P-SA	P-T					T-T
M.8	The Technology Façade			P-T	T-H	T-S		T-L	T-T
M.9	Impact of Technology on Student Achievement			P-T				T-L	T-T
M.10	Faculty Experiences with Instructional Technology			P-T				T-L	T-T
M.11	Constantly Changing Technology World			P-T			T-SA	T-L	T-T

See Appendix E for Skills/Competencies and Learning Outcomes

P-C   Pedagogy - Content knowledge
P-SA Pedagogy - Skills Acquisition
P-T   Pedagogy - Teaching competence
T-H   Technology - Hardware
T-S   Technology - Software
T-SA Technology - Skills Acquisition
T-L   Technology - Learning
T-T   Technology - Teaching

Figure 6.6 **The Skills and Competencies of the Master Integrator.** *Source*: Author-developed for this book.

connotes a growing confidence with one's pedagogical skills and a need to increase his or her use of technology. (T)*echnological Integrator* essentially is the opposite of the pedagogical expert, is an individual rapidly developing expertise with technology but needs to refine pedagogy. (J)*ourneyman Integrators* might best be described as a jack-of-both-trades (pedagogy and technology) but a master of neither, while (M)a*ster Integrator* is our ultimate destination, attaining comfort and proficiency on both axes.

Nearly 70 teaching episodes are offered in this chapter and Appendix D. Certainly, we have not recognized all possible topics that go into making an effective college or university faculty member. So, we provide readers with a template (Appendix E) for creating even more episodes. We encourage you to expand the list as you see fit and share your descriptions, learning outcomes, skills, and competencies with other contributors on our personal learning network (see chapter 10).

Chapter 7

Determining Your Location on the Integrated Readiness Matrix

7.1. INTRODUCTION

The process of plotting an initial location on the X–Y grid allows faculty to assess where they are and where they need to improve with respect to their pedagogical and technological preparations. The steps provided in this chapter lead faculty toward their goal of becoming a Master Integrator. They can pattern a professional development program, drawing on many resources recommended in this text where like-minded and similarly capable faculty interact.

7.2. CONDUCTING A PERSONAL SELF-ASSESSMENT
(A Subjective Estimation of Your Location on the IRM)

Let's use a practical example of how two different college faculty members go about estimating where they are on the Integrated Readiness Matrix (IRM). The first colleague, Faculty-Member-A, is a part-time undergraduate faculty of University A's School of Liberal Arts. The second colleague, Faculty-Member-B, is a full-time graduate faculty in the School of Education at the same institution.

7.2.1. Determine Your Level of Teaching in the Pedagogical Domain

Recognize your dominant level of teaching in the pedagogical domain. Faculty-Member-A gathers recent syllabi from offerings of his *Introduction to Psychology* course he teaches every semester. He begins by focusing on his stated learning objectives (sometimes referred to as learning goals or learning outcomes). Faculty-Member B mirrors her colleague's efforts, collecting

Level of Bloom's Revised Taxonomy	Common Action Verbs
I. Remembering. Exhibit memory of previously learned material by recalling facts, terms, basic concepts, and answers.	Choose, Define, Find, How, Label, List, Match, Name, Recall, Relate, Select, Show, Spell, What, When, Where, Which, Who, Why
II. Understanding. Demonstrate understanding of facts and ideas by organizing, comparing, translating, interpreting, giving descriptions, and stating main ideas.	Classify, Compare, Contrast, Demonstrate, Explain, Illustrate, Infer, Interpret, Outline, Relate, Rephrase, Summarize, Translate
III. Applying. Solve problems to new situations by applying acquired knowledge, facts, techniques and rules in a different way.	Apply, Build, Choose, Construct, Develop, Identify, Interview, Use, Model, Organize, Plan, Select, Solve, Utilize
IV. Analyzing. Examine and deconstruct information into parts. Make inferences and find evidence to support generalizations.	Analyze, Assume, Categorize, Classify, Compare, Conclusion, Contrast, Discover, Dissect, Distinguish, Divide, Examine, Infer, Inspect, List, Relate, Simplify, Survey, Test
V. Evaluating. Present and defend opinions by making judgments about information, validity of ideas, or quality of work based on a set of criteria.	Agree, Appraise, Argue, Assess, Choose, Compare, Conclude, Criticize, Decide, Deduce, Defend, Determine, Disprove, Estimate, Evaluate, Explain, Interpret, Judge, Justify, Measure, Prioritize, Prove, Rate, Recommend, Select, Support, Value
VI. Creating. Gather information together in new and different ways by combining elements in a new pattern or proposing alternative solutions.	Adapt, Build, Change, Combine, Compile, Compose, Construct, Create, Delete, Design, Develop, Formulate, Imagine, Improve, Invent, Modify, Originate, Plan, Predict, Propose, Solve, Suppose, Test

Figure 7.1 Pedagogical Action Verbs. *Source*: Author-developed for this book.

objectives from her graduate course in *Foundations of Online Teaching and Learning*.

Match the pedagogical learning objectives to Bloom's Taxonomy. Uncovering the level of Bloom's Taxonomy is accomplished by comparing the objectives found in each syllabus to a list of commonly accepted pedagogical action verbs such as those shown in Figure 7.1.

Faculty-Member-A makes a good faith effort to label each objective found in his *Psychology* course as shown in Figure 7.2. Faculty-Member-B will do likewise with *Foundations of Online Teaching and Learning* (Figure 7.3).

7.2.2. Determine Your Level of Teaching in the Technological Domain

The same pattern is repeated; this time Faculty-Member-A and Faculty-Member-B focus on technological objectives found in their respective syllabi.

Recognize your dominant level of teaching in the technological domain. Faculty-Member-A identifies his technology-focused learning objectives from his syllabi. Faculty-Member B does the same for her graduate course.

Determining Your Location on the Integrated Readiness Matrix 69

Objective	Example Learning Objective Taken from Syllabi	Enter Bloom's Level Here
1	Define psychology and identify the various functions of psychological theory/practice.	Remembering
2	Employ the scientific method as it is applied to a instructor-provided real-world situation reflecting the study of human behavior.	Applying
3	Demonstrate various theories of psychology as they relate to human development.	Understanding
4	Explain the relationship between biology and behavior.	Understanding
5	Compare and contrast the higher-order mental abilities such as learning, memory, language, and thought.	Understanding
6	Use a model provided by the instructor that displays the effects of stress upon emotional/physical health and psychological methods for reducing stress.	Applying
7	Explain motivation and emotion-based influences on behavior.	Understanding
8	Describe many of the social influences on human behavior.	Understanding
9	Define abnormality with regard to human behavior and describe different therapeutic approaches used to treat psychological dysfunction.	Remembering

Figure 7.2 Classifying Pedagogical Learning Objectives (Undergraduate Course). *Source*: Author-developed for this book.

Objective	Example Learning Objective Taken from Syllabi	Enter Bloom's Level Here
1	Apply concepts of basic technology problem-solving related to satisfying course requirements; history of distance learning; and, introduction to learning theories.	Applying
2	Appreciate the online learning experience from the perspective of a student, including students with special needs in the online classroom.	Analyzing
3	Apply basic pedagogies related to distance education and the use of various technology-based instructional strategies,	Applying
4	Experience practical, hands-on encounters in the application and implementation of technology in the online environment.	Evaluating
5	Organize a series of online activities reflecting actual online learning situations into a cohesive online lesson.	Applying
6	Analyze the components of a course management system and identify viable learning events; instructional sequence; and, possible technology-based instructional materials for an online lesson curriculum.	Analyzing
7	Conduct an assessment of learning objectives as they apply to online teaching and learning and design online assessment tools (e.g., Grade Book software, online objective tests, authentic electronic portfolios) to ensure learning has occurred.	Evaluating

Figure 7.3 Classifying Pedagogical Learning Objectives (Graduate Course). *Source*: Author-developed for this book.

Match the technological learning objectives to Tomei's Taxonomy. Uncovering the respective level of Tomei's Taxonomy is similarly straightforward. Compare each objective found in the syllabus to a list of commonly accepted technological action verbs shown in Figure 7.4.

Level of Tomei's Taxonomy	Action Verbs *
Literacy. Minimum degree of competency expected of teachers and students	Capture digital pictures Download and incorporate text and images Electronically transfer files Employ search engines Navigate educational software Open, save, close, drag files Share files Save/store selected files
Collaboration. Using technology to share ideas	Communicate information digitally Edit, revise, and resubmit a research paper Email communications with parents/families **Participate in a chat session/ bulletin board** Share information electronically
Decision-making. Solving problems	Decide using spreadsheet analyses Develop decision support systems Interpret charts/graphs Track student progress via grade book software
Learning with Technology. Infusing technology into the learning process	Adapt technologies to academic standards Add links to classroom websites Conduct digital research Explore selected web-based sites Harvest (download) digital content
Teaching with Technology. Integrating teacher-made, technology-based resources	Create a slide presentation Generate a narrated slide show Produce a Hyperbook Produce an Interactive Lesson
Tech-ology. The study of technology	Address issues of technology access inequities Advocate for and against issues of technology Set policy for computer usage and Internet access Recognize human/social factors that affect technology use

Figure 7.4 Technological Action Verbs (Tomei, 2005). *Source*: Author-developed for this book.

Determining Your Location on the Integrated Readiness Matrix 71

Objective	Example Learning Objective Taken from Syllabi	Enter Tomei's Level Here
A	Understand the benefits of a multi-disciplinary, media-based approach to psychology	Literacy
B	Students will be able to correctly describe the personal and society-wide beliefs and biases toward media and technology	Collaboration
C	Students will post their personal journals weekly with peers using the discussion board and e-mail with the faculty.	Collaboration
D	Students will demonstrate An understanding of the psychological underpinnings of media literacy and digital citizenship.	Literacy
E	Students will use the Socrates app available on mobile smart phones to explore real-world exercises and identify psychological conditions of simulated subjects.	Decision-making
F	Students will use simulation software to design, build, and test solutions to real-world problems. Is there a distinction between online and offline in how we communicate and make meaning of the world around us?	Decision-making
G	Students will discuss how a globally networked world influences our understanding of others and ourselves.	Collaboration

Figure 7.5 Classifying Pedagogical Learning Objectives (Undergraduate Course). *Source*: Author-developed for this book.

Objective	Example Learning Objective Taken from Syllabi	Tomei's Level Entered Here
A	Implement personalized and effective methods of managing an online course.	Learning with Technology
B	Prepare an interactive lesson that advocates for the basic legal issues of teaching online.	Teaching with Technology
C	Collaborate with others in the digital learning environment. Facilitate an online discussion.	Collaboration
D	Use the spreadsheet provided by the instructor to weigh the important concepts of such as copyright, accessibility and open educational resources to the digital learning environment.	Decision-making
E	Demonstrate use of various collaboration methods and technological tools in the design of online course materials.	Learning with Technology
F	Utilize WWW (World Wide Web)-based resources to support specific learning objectives and outcomes.	Learning with Technology
G	Apply learning and instructional design theories to the design and implementation of a successful blended or online course.	Teaching with Technology
H	Interpret learning management system skills and technology skills required of instructors in the online classroom.	Decision-making

Figure 7.6 Faculty-Member-B's Technological Learning Objectives from her Graduate Foundations of Online Teaching and Learning Course Syllabus. *Source*: Author-developed for this book.

As before, Faculty-Member-A labels each objective found in his *Introductory Course in Psychology* course (Figure 7.5.). Faculty-Member-B will do likewise with her *Foundations of Online Teaching and Learning* (Figure 7.6.).

7.2.3. Plot Your Learning Objectives on the IRM

Place each learning objective in the respective matrix cell to extrapolate the quadrant that best fits the integration of pedagogy and technology.

Figure 7.7. shows the *pedagogical 1-9* learning objectives and *technological A-G* objectives for Faculty-Member-A. As a relatively junior part-time faculty member, most of his learning objectives would likely be located in the bottom-left quadrant. Faculty-Member-A categorized himself as an Apprentice Integrator of pedagogy and technology.

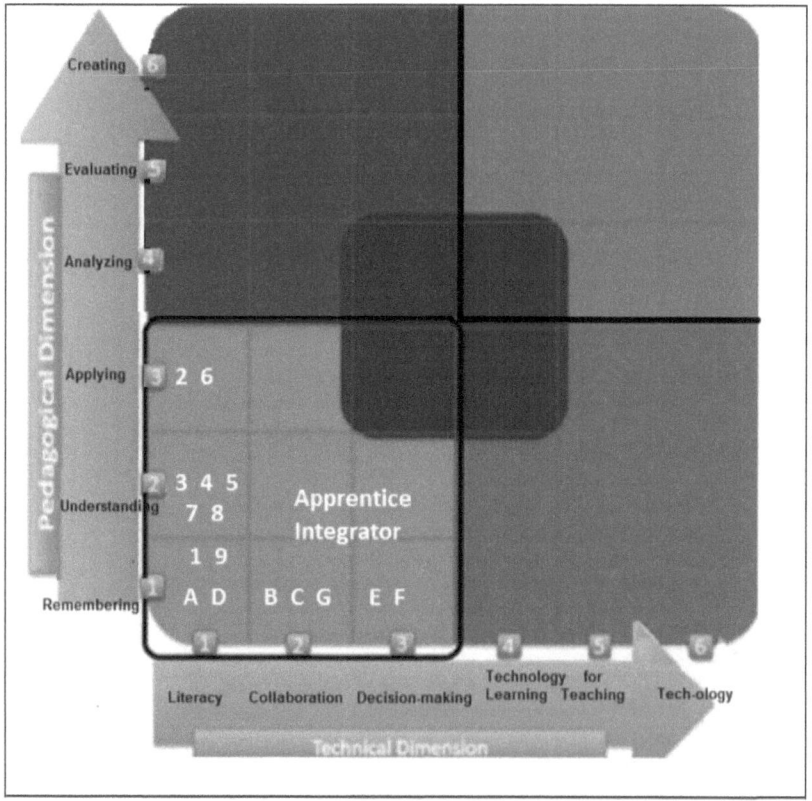

Figure 7.7 Faculty-Member-A Self-Identified on the Integrated Readiness Matrix.
Note that for this taxonomy, a single underline denotes the action verb and a double underline suggests an appropriate technology for that level of the taxonomy. *Source*: Author-developed for this book.

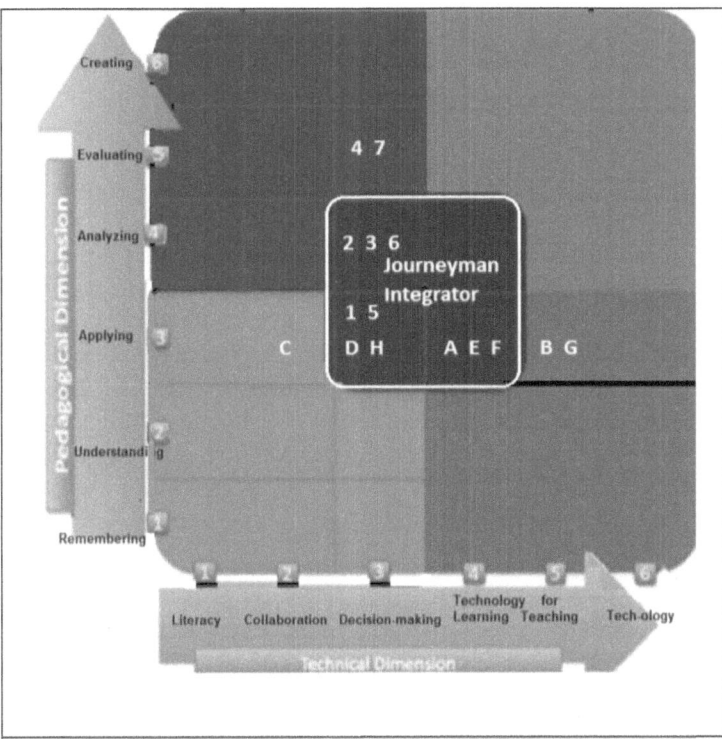

Figure 7.8 Faculty-Member-B Self-Identified on the Integrated Readiness Matrix.
Source: Author-developed for this book.

Figure 7.8. shows the results for Faculty-Member-B. She is a more senior faculty member. As such, her learning objectives are more broadly distributed, especially her technological objectives. Based on the results of a review of her syllabi objectives, Faculty-Member-B identifies herself as a Journeyman Integrator of pedagogy and technology.

Summary. Do not expect a perfect fit of all learning objectives into a single quadrant of the matrix. There are bound to be some outliers as skills and competencies found in Chapter 6 are developed.

7.3. COMPLETE THE IRM SURVEY INSTRUMENT
(Objective Assessment of Your Location on the Matrix)

So far, we have conducted a *subjective* self-review. The two hypothetical colleagues from a fictional university were asked to select a course (or courses) of their choice, isolate learning objectives from syllabi, and compare them to a list of action verbs to plot a location on the matrix grid.

In this section of the chapter, we offer higher education faculty member a more *objective* assessment instrument to gage where you truly are on the IRM.

7.3.1. Complete the Survey Instrument

The authors have closely examined the domains of pedagogy and technology. A blank copy of the instrument is provided in Appendix F so it can be removed and used by the reader. We will walk through its use in a few simple steps.

Complete the *pedagogical* learning objectives found in the survey instrument. The instrument itself is designed as a forced-choice tool. Use the same pedagogical learning objectives found in the syllabi used earlier for the self-assessment. Faculty who teach more than one course may include additional objectives from the wider range of courses represented in their teaching load. Follow these instructions and then proceed.

1. Read each pair of objectives and select only one objective that best describes the learning objective would *most likely* be found in your own syllabus;
2. Place a check in the box next to the objective selected;
3. Do not attempt to decipher which is the better objective or which objective you would prefer to teach; instead, identify the objective that would *most likely be found in your own teaching plans*;
4. Do not be concerned with subject-matter areas expressed in the survey as the instrument includes objectives from diverse content areas; instead, focus on the perceived *level* of the pedagogical taxonomy.

The practical example of how Faculty-Member-A and Faculty-Member-B might complete the instrument will continue to demonstrate the objectives scoring of the survey instrument. Assume the instrument in Appendix F was completed and the following objectives checked by Faculty-Member-A (Figure 7.9.). The Points Awarded (Column PA) for each matched pair of objectives produces *Total Pedagogical Points Awarded of 71 points* for Faculty-Member-A.

Compare the *technological* learning objectives found in the survey instrument. The same review process focuses on technological objectives found in each syllabus. The result: for Faculty-Member-A, the matched pair of objectives produces *Total Technological Points Awarded 77 points* (Figure 7.10).

Determining Your Location on the Integrated Readiness Matrix 75

Faculty-Member-A chose this pedagogical learning objective (excerpt provided) as most closely matching an objective in his syllabi....	✓	PA
01b. After completing the class activities for the day, the student will ...	✓	3
02a. Students will be able to correctly name the major bones...	✓	1
3a. Given a series of polygons, the student will correctly distinguish ...	✓	2
04a. Students will prepare a treatment strategy based on ...	✓	3
05a. After completing the lesson, the student will discriminate the ...	✓	4
06a. Students will evaluate staffing assignments ...	✓	5
07a. Students will list five criteria for the evaluation of ...	✓	1
08a. After this unit, the student will distinguish among types of ...	✓	2
09b. Given the results of relevant tests for determining heart-related ...	✓	5
10a. Students will differentiate among the passages that attack ...	✓	4
11a. Students will compare and contrast the most effective treatments ...	✓	5
12b. Students will demonstrate the principle of reinforcement ...	✓	5
13a. Students will paraphrase the meanings of the 4 basic principles ...	✓	3
14a. After completing the lesson, students will be able to solve ...	✓	4
15b. Candidates will devise a yearly plan with staff ...	✓	8
16a. Candidates will label at least three unique ways to ...	✓	2
17a. Given the geological ages of rock formations, students will ...	✓	3
18a. Students will offer a 3-5 minute demonstration of how ...	✓	4
19a. Students will list all 7 steps involved in locating the epicenter ...	✓	2
20a. After completing the activities, students will use organized data ...	✓	3
21a. Students will articulate the characteristics of each type of ...	✓	2
Total Pedagogical Points Awarded		71

Figure 7.9 Faculty-Member-A's Pedagogical Learning Objectives from the Survey Instrument. *Source*: Author-developed for this book.

Determine the X,Y coordinate and plot those coordinates on the IRM to determine the quadrant. Use the scale provided in Table 7.9 to plot the x- and y-coordinates on the IRM. The table provides the results of an extended pilot study of a significant population of faculty and how they performed on the instrument in relation to the normal curve (Bernauer, Davis, and Tomei, 2012).

For Faculty-Member-A, the instrument produced a technological (X-axis) score of 77 points. Table 7.1. converts that score into an *X-coordinate of 3*.

Faculty-Member-A chose this technological learning objective (excerpt provided) as most closely matching an objective in his syllabi....	✓	PA
01a. Students will be able to select, load, and play age-appropriate ...	✓	1
02b. Students will use technology to enhance their skills for ...	✓	3
03b. Students will use technology as a data gathering tool to ...	✓	4
04a. Students will use technology to think critically and solve ...	✓	3
05a. Students will participate in technology-based projects and ...	✓	4
06a. Teachers will create the core of an online course, including ...	✓	5
07a. Students will demonstrate proper use and care of ...	✓	1
08b. The teacher will provide instructional databases to ...	✓	4
09b. Educators will be introduced to the necessary technologies ...	✓	5
10b. Educators will access curriculum materials from a variety of ...	✓	6
11a. Students will design, develop, prototype, and exhibit ...	✓	5
12a. Students will be able to correctly match at least 10 hardware ...	✓	2
13b. Students will work cooperatively using email and ...	✓	6
14b. Videotape a fellow student using the new Apple iPad device ...	✓	7
15a. After identifying the key characteristics of the greatest battle, ...	✓	5
16a. Students will gather information using at least 4 different ...	✓	2
17a. Teachers will communicate at least weekly with students using ...	✓	3
18a. Contrasting weather data from last fall, winter, and spring, ...	✓	4
19a. The library/media centers within our school will become ...	✓	2
20a. Students will interact synchronously (via online chat rooms) ...	✓	3
21a. Students will utilize developmentally appropriate instructional ...	✓	2
Total Technological Points Awarded		77

Figure 7.10 Faculty-Member-A's Technological Learning Objectives from the Survey Instrument. *Source*: Author-developed for this book.

Table 7.1 Determining Coordinates on the IRM

Normal curve	Technology score	X-coordinate	Pedagogy score	Y-coordinate
0.02	61–63	1	61–63	1
0.135	64–75.34	2	64–75.34	2
0.34	75.35–96.5	3	75.35–96.5	3
0.34	96.51–117.64	4	96.51–117.64	4
0.135	117.65–131	5	117.65–131	5
0.02	132–133	6	132–133	6

Determining Your Location on the Integrated Readiness Matrix 77

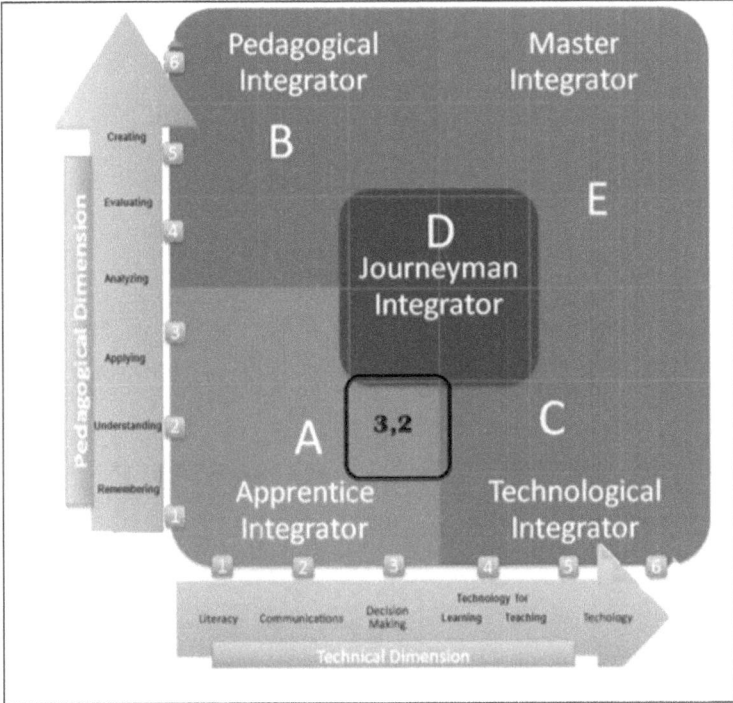

Figure 7.11 Plotting Faculty-Member-A Survey Instrument Coordinates on the IRM.
Source: Author-developed for this book.

The pedagogical (Y-axis) score of 71 points is converted to a *Y-coordinate of 2*. Therefore, the coordinates for the IRM would be 3,2 (Figure 7.11).

7.3.2. Validating the Results

The survey instrument places Faculty-Member-A on the IRM matrix at coordinates (3,2), inside the Apprentice Integrator quadrant, precisely where he self-identified in the earlier exercise. Further, when compared side-by-side (Figure 7.12), it would appear that Faculty-Member-B, who is perhaps just beginning a career as a college instructor, is ready to move from Apprentice integrator to Journeyman to Master Integrator (note the commas).

Next, compare the results for Faculty-Member-B following the same steps.

Compare the *pedagogical* learning objectives found in the survey instrument. Recapping the Maximum Points Recommended in Column PR to the Points Awarded in Column PA as for each matched pair of objectives produces *Total Pedagogical Points Awarded 94 points* for Faculty-Member-B. From here, we will omit the respective tables for brevity. Trust us!

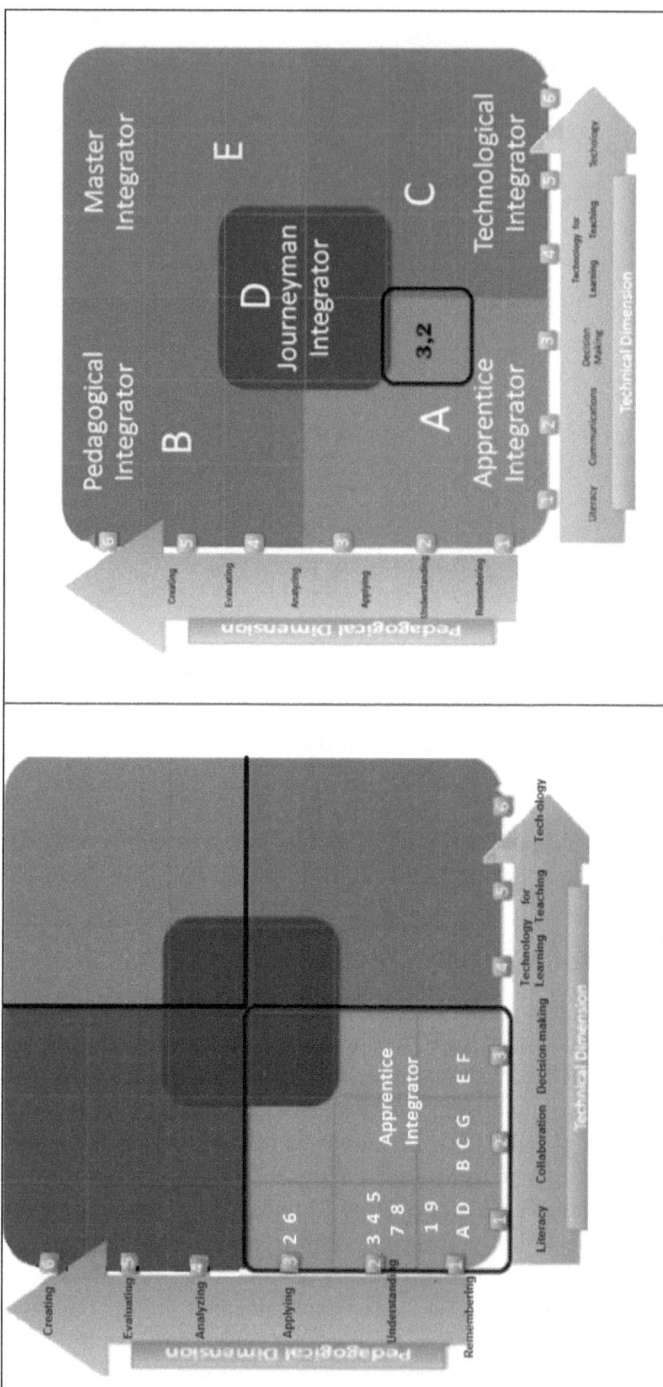

Figure 7.12 Compare Faculty-Member-A Self-Assessment with the Survey Instrument. *Source:* Author-developed for this book.

Compare the *technological* learning objectives found in your syllabi to the survey instrument. The matched pair of objectives produces *Total Technological Points Awarded 113 points* for Faculty-Member-B.

Determine the X,Y coordinate and plot those coordinates on the IRM to determine the quadrant. For Faculty-Member-B, the instrument produced a technological (X-axis) score of 113 points; an *X-coordinate of 4*. The pedagogical (Y-axis) score of 94 points is converted to a *Y-coordinate of 3* (Table 7.2.). Therefore, the coordinates for the IRM would be 4,3 (Figure 7.13).

Table 7.2 Determining Coordinates on the IRM

Normal curve	Technology score	X-coordinate	Pedagogy score	Y-coordinate
0.02	61–63	1	61–63	1
0.135	64–75.34	2	64–75.34	2
0.34	75.35–96.5	3	75.35–96.5	3
0.34	96.51–117.64	4	96.51–117.64	4
0.135	117.65–131	5	117.65–131	5
0.02	132–133	6	132–133	6

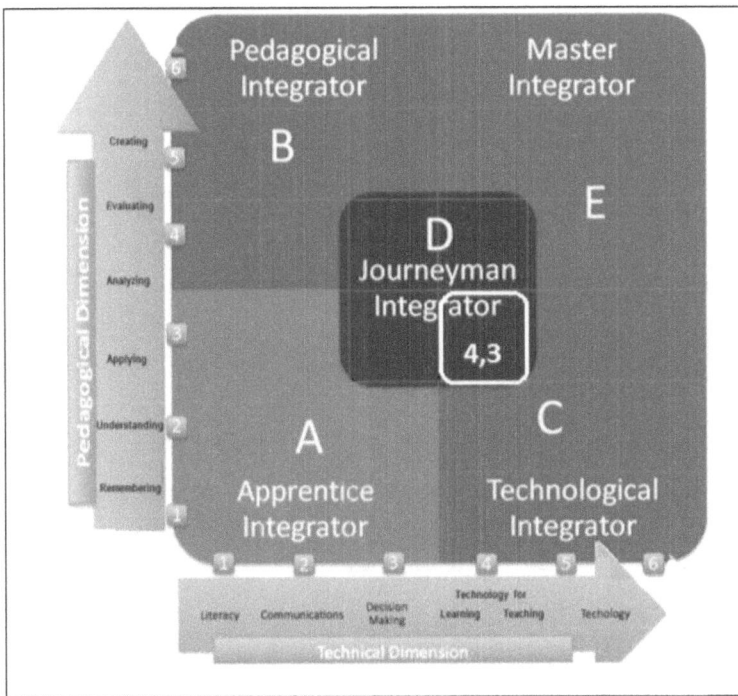

Figure 7.13 Plotting Faculty-Member-B Survey Instrument Coordinates on the IRM.
Source: Author-developed for this book.

80   Chapter 7

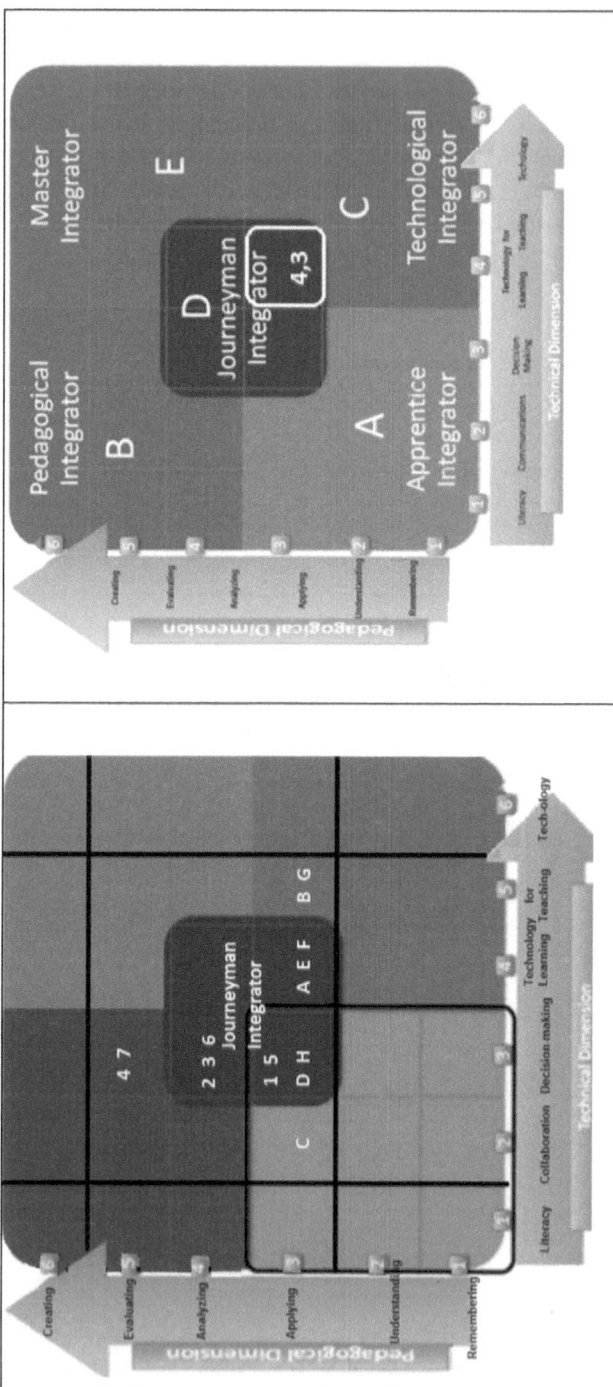

Figure 7.14 Compare Faculty-Member-B Self-Assessment with the Survey Instrument. *Source:* Author-developed for this book.

7.3.4. Validating the Results

The survey instrument places Faculty-Member-B on the IRM matrix at coordinates (4,3), inside the Journeyman Integrator quadrant; again, in close proximity to where she previously self-identified. When further compared side-by-side (Figure 7.14), it would appear that Faculty-Member-B is further along in her career of becoming a master integrator.

7.4. CONCLUSION

So, what happens if the two assessments result in placements in different quadrants? While the two faculty members placed them solidly in one of the five quadrants, it is often the case that the pedagogical and technological objectives are more scattered throughout the matrix. If that occurs, the short answer is to rely on the instrument that places you in the *more conservative* quadrant.

Suppose, for example, that the survey instrument placed you in Quadrant A as an Apprentice Integrator but you rated yourself a Quadrant D Journeyman Integrator. Since the purpose of this text is to develop faculty members as integrators of both pedagogy and technology so that they ultimately become Master Integrators, it makes sense to begin your journey in the more conservative posture, that is, Quadrant A. Faculty would be better served to accept their mastery of skills at the lower level rather than experience frustration and disappointment trying to tackle competencies that may still be beyond their reach.

REFERENCES

Bernauer, James A., Davis, Christopher T., and Tomei, Lawrence A. (2012). Integrated Readiness Matrix: A Synergy of Pedagogy and Technology for Educational Leadership. *Technology and Its Impact on Educational Leadership: Innovation and Change* by Victor C.X. Wang, Hershey, PA: IGI Global.

Dunn, Jeff (2014), The 6 Levels of Bloom's Taxonomy, Explained with Active Verbs. URL: http://www.edudemic.com/the-6-levels-of-blooms-taxonomy/

Tomei, Lawrence A. Taxonomy for the Technology Domain: A Classification of Educational Objectives for the Technology Domain, Idea Group Publishers, Inc. 2005.

Part IV

DEVELOPING/IMPROVING A CENTER FOR TEACHING EXCELLENCE

Part Four removes the theoretical glasses that were used to examine the foundational concepts of teaching and learning, technology, culture, and the Integrated Readiness Matrix (IRM). In the remaining chapters, we don a more practical, real-world perspective to guide readers to develop or improve a Center for Teaching Excellence at their respective institutions.

Here, we examine how the Center for Innovative Teaching and Directed Engaged Learning (CITADEL) developed at Robert Morris University (RMU).

Box Part IV.1

> Remain alert to our Best Practices windows. The authors are offering the successes (and misadventures) of the CITADEL over its first three years since its inauguration as a center for excellence at RMU. Pay particular attention to the highlighted boxes.

The chapters in Part Four are a case study of the initial three years of the RMU CITADEL in hopes that our successes and failures can serve others. We explain how various workshops fit into the IRM, review lessons learned, and offer suggestions for other university leaders in planning a similar teaching center.

Finally, we offer an invitation to you and your colleagues to join us in discussing how to enhance pedagogy and technology.

Chapter 8

Building a Center for Teaching Excellence

8.1 INTRODUCTION

The Center for Innovative Teaching and Directed Engaged Learning (CITADEL) at Robert Morris University(RMU) was formally approved in the summer of 2013. Its organizational structure combined two components: the Office of Innovative Teaching (OIT) and the Office of Directed Engaged Learning (DEL).

The two components are complementary, both targeting our institution's core values of *academic excellence* and *engaged student learning*. The CITADEL officially opened its doors for the 2013–14 academic year, although not fully operational. In its initial year, the OIT delivered multiple faculty workshops and programs using the Integrated Readiness Matrix (IRM) as its implementation model. The OIT took as its germinal challenge to review the pedagogical challenges and opportunities that exist within higher education; explore how technological tools can aid in teaching; and share common teaching and learning experiences among colleagues.

In Year 2, more university-specific programs were added and a new online faculty community was formed. All faculty be they full-time or part-time, new to higher education or a seasoned veteran, engineer or accountant were encouraged to embrace the CITADEL's offerings. Taking what they

Box 8.1

All faculty, full-time or part-time, new to higher education or seasoned veteran, engineer, or accountant, were encouraged to embrace the CITADEL's offerings. Taking what they experienced at workshops and incorporating these experiences into their own classes benefit students and further develops faculty.

experienced at workshops and incorporating these experiences into their own classes benefits students and further develops faculty.

The Office of Directed Engaged Learning was the realization of our former university president. Since 2009, RMU on-ground students must meet Student Engagement Transcript (SET) requirements in order to graduate. There are six SET categories: arts, culture, creativity; transcultural/global experiences; undergraduate research; service; leadership; and professional experience. (See Appendix G, description of SET categories.) Students must complete two of the six as a graduation requirement. Those who complete all six categories and receive special recognition for undergraduate experience (e.g., selected for Dean's List) earn the Renaissance Award. SET opportunities often include a faculty member in the role of mentor, advisor, or instructor – another advantage of combining Innovative Teaching and Engaged Directed Learning.

CITADEL offices are led by full-time faculty coordinators who retain their status within the university's faculty union. Coordinators receive a one-course teaching load reduction per semester and a stipend. These nine-month appointments were designed to deliver upon one of the CITADEL's promises: faculty involvement in its operation. The director has a 12-month appointment and also receives a stipend.

Box 8.2

> The director has a 12-month appointment and receives a stipend. Center coordinators have a nine-month appointment and receive a one-course teaching load reduction per semester and a stipend.

The CITADEL did not reach its personnel staffing plan in its initial year of operation. A faculty coordinator was identified for Innovative Teaching and she assumed that role after a semester-length Fulbright assignment overseas. Finding an Engaged Learning coordinator proved to be more difficult and was later abandoned. The director of the CITADEL assumed the coordinator responsibilities and continues in the dual role.

Engaged Learning is staffed by an assistant director and an engaged learning specialist. Figure 8.1. below shows the administrative structure of the CITADEL. Advisory boards were later established for both offices.

8.2. INAUGURAL YEAR (2013–14)

Buy-in. Buy-in. Buy-in. Among the challenges with a new initiative such as the CITADEL is ensuring buy-in from faculty, staff, and administrators

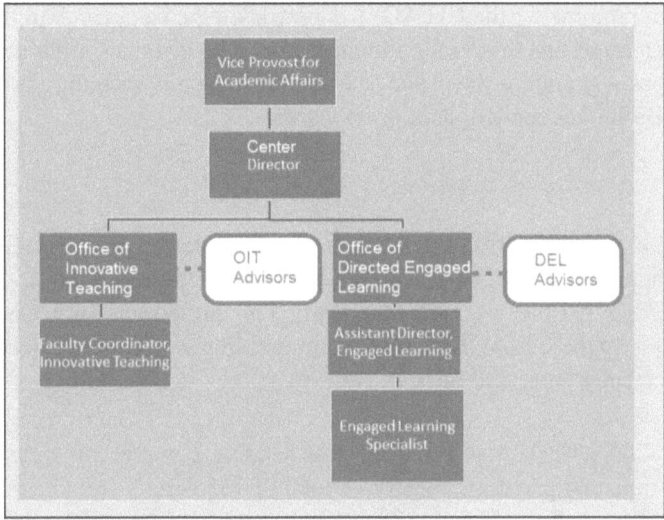

Figure 8.1 Organizational Structure of a Center for Teaching Excellence. *Source*: Author-developed for this book.

across the campus. A center of excellence is an idea to which many people give that instant nod of approval, but the goal should be ensuring that as many people as possible know what the center is doing and want to find their place in it. This is especially true when the center is in its initial semester on campus. During this brief time, there is ample opportunity for people to get involved because the formation of the mission, vision, and purpose are still in their infancy.

Box 8.3

Ensure buy-in from faculty, staff, and administrators across the campus. There is ample opportunity for people to get involved because the formation of the mission, vision, and purpose are still in their infancy.

To that end, the center director and the assistant director of Engaged Learning visited every RMU academic unit during the fall term. They explained the purpose of the CITADEL, laid out preliminary goals for the upcoming academic year, solicited input for semester events, and restated the role of academic units in its development. Questions included evaluating student work as it related to the SET, enhancing student engagement opportunities, identifying courses that fit well with the current SET, and more. A smile and an affirmation ensured that their message was received and appreciated. Careful attention was placed not to judge the reception rather to acknowledge that the message was being heard across the campus. This turned out to be essential in ramping up the CITADEL's profile on the campus. And this also serves as an important lesson for administrators who begin a similar center on their campus – get out of the office and into those faculty meetings as soon as possible. Build that needed identity on campus.

Box 8.4

> Leaders of the CITADEL should visit every academic unit periodically. Careful attention should be placed not to judge the reception but rather to acknowledge that the message was heard. This turned out to be essential in ramping up the CITADEL's profile on the campus. Get out of the office and into faculty early and often.

One of CITADEL's first successes was sending a university-wide survey to all full-time and part-time faculty. A total of 135 faculty from each of five schools participated. Responses were largely anecdotal but still an important barometer of faculty interest in developing their pedagogical skills. It was not a surprise that two of every three respondents were part-time faculty or assistant professors. This segment of the faculty often feels they are separate from their full-time colleagues. Assistant professors often concentrate on the intricacies of teaching as quickly as possible because of tenure and promotion. Each, therefore, saw the CITADEL and its offerings as a chance to become more involved in the campus life, interact with colleagues outside the classroom, and enhance their pedagogical skills.

The principal purpose of the survey was to gage faculty interest in a host of professional development opportunities. The workshop ideas that drew the most support centered on teaching and research. Because the CITADEL focuses on teaching, workshops highlighting pedagogy were identified.

Box 8.5

> Administer a university-wide survey to all full-time and part-time faculty. The principal purpose of the survey is to gage faculty interest in a host of professional development opportunities.

8.3. YEAR TWO (2014–15)

Appendix H suggests where all CITADEL-sponsored programs for both Years 2 and 3 fit into the IRM matrix. CITADEL workshops often employed a flipped classroom approach. See chapter 1 (para 1.2.5. *The Connectivist Classroom)*, for more information about flipped classrooms). Attendees were frequently given a link to webinars to prepare for face-to-face interactions. Workshops resembled graduate-level seminars: conversations focused on multiple items that often built upon each other and challenged each participant to make a meaningful contribution. No single consensus came out of the programs, though the attendees acknowledged that setting expectations for the class in the first week, meaningfully incorporating the right kind of technology whenever possible into the course, and encouraging students to consider ethical practices in their decision-making were essential in establishing a mindset that hard work was expected and would be rewarded.

A workshop presented the basics of a flipped classroom as a teaching strategy. Faculty across the university gathered for a *Chronicle of Higher Education* webinar on the topic. However, the webinar focused more on how technology plays an important role in the success of a flipped classroom approach. One of its essential points, creating 5–7 minute videos, later became one of the central talking points. Attendees appreciated learning that simply recording their standard 50–75 minute would not serve their students well. Chunking was recommended practice allowing for a critical theme to be presented in a few short videos rather than in one long video.

Two programs were also delivered as webinars by outside agencies. The first was hosted by NVivo and looked at how it provides powerful software for qualitative data analysis that also helps make insight-driven decisions. One of the attendees had been using NVivo in her classroom and for her research. She agreed to create a handbook that detailed how to use the software, its teaching applications, and more. Here again is evidence of the value of empowering the faculty to take the lead on projects that contribute to their teaching, research or service, and that benefit the entire campus community. Later, an *Inside Higher Ed* webinar reviewed its most recent poll of faculty opinions about technology.

CITADEL-sponsored events continued to be offered during the academic year. The addition of the Innovative Teaching faculty coordinator was essential in nearly doubling the number of programs. An especially well-attended workshop examined academic integrity issues such as the culture of cheating in colleges. The involvement of three RMU students who were part of the university's Academic Integrity Council was a particularly well-received addition. As the head of that council noted, students often are less tolerant of cheating and demand stiffer penalties than faculty. Later, a program about academic integrity and online classes was held. Attendees were introduced to the lockdown browsers and online monitors. A critical takeaway that came from this workshop found that regardless of faculty attention to prevent cheating, technology seems determined to make this an ongoing issue into the future.

A critical focus on teaching occurred during Year 2. A *Chronicle of Higher Education* webinar sponsored by the CITADEL reviewed how e-portfolios can be used by faculty and students. Another program focused on disconnects between faculty and students when it comes to course assignments and instructor feedback. A white paper published by Turnitin served as the jumping off point to this seminar, which also included one of the paper's authors participating via videoconference.

The signature event of the second year was a roundtable panel hosted by previous University Teaching Award winners. In this session, three faculty members explored how they motivate and engage their students in the classroom. The business faculty detailed how role playing scenarios in which students assume the position of a union leader and a company president demand a level of preparation and focus on professional skills that students typically do not receive in lecture-based classes. The nursing faculty member highlighted how he gives students an exam then clusters them in small groups to review the questions. Those groups are then allowed to submit the exam again. If their group score is higher than the highest individual score from that group, then everyone receives a bonus score that is credited at the end of the term.

Box 8.6

The signature event of the second year was a roundtable panel hosted by previous University Teaching Award winners. Use your own faculty to deliver presentations.

Further along in Year 2, the focus turned to outcomes assessment, an issue gaining in importance throughout the country. The program was designed to be conversational; RMU faculty who had adopted interesting assessment tools for the classroom offered their models for consideration. Following those presentations, discussions ranged from clarifying terminology to understanding accrediting agency mandates.

App-reciating the App was our final program for Year 2. Faculty were encouraged to discuss and demonstrate their favorite smart phone application for teaching.

The creation of Personal Learning Networks (PLNs) as an aftermath of each workshop session was a goal. But during our first year, only one was created that focused on student writing. The PLN was moderately successful with a faculty member as its head and approximately 10 members sharing ideas. Regular threads were posed as questions, akin to what might be done in an online course. Members were encouraged to discuss ways to evaluate written student work. One of the goals for Year 3 was to expand the PLNs. They offer an impressive resource for faculty to discuss important pedagogical issues.

Box 8.7

Create PLNs after each workshop to encourage continued discussion among interested faculty and keep important conversations moving forward.

8.4. INTERIM ACTIVITIES

Before the end of the second year of the program, faculty were introduced to the IRM. Some centers opted to conduct a single-themed workshop to introduce the IRM; others provided their faculty with copies of *Integrating Pedagogy and Technology: Improving Teaching and Learning in Higher Education* (Bernauer & Tomei, 2015). Now that this text is published, you may wish to substitute this higher education-specific focus of the IRM instead.

During the summer hiatus between the second and third years, the center administered the IRM Instrument (Chapter 7, Appendix F). Center leadership took advantage of the summer break to review the results and track faculty by quadrant. The upcoming academic year would see many more center-sponsored events. The IRM instrument would allow faculty to be placed in developmentally appropriate workshops.

Box 8.8

Administer the IRM instrument upon conclusion of the second year of the center's implementation. If your center is already established, you may administer the instrument at your discretion. Use the results of the survey to place faculty in upcoming pedagogical and technological workshops.

Box 8.9

Do *not* request copies of the completed survey instrument from the faculty. This will impede acceptance of the results and tend to inflate where faculty place themselves in the matrix. Instead, request only the quadrant identified by the faculty member.

Box 8.10

Use survey results from Year 3 and beyond to place faculty in future workshops. Administer the survey instrument in each of the following years.

8.5. YEAR 3 (2015–16)

The academic year began with an important shift in programming: internally produced events would dominate the calendar. Use of webinars and externally sponsored events would be reduced. Creating local programs was the natural by-product of attending the New Faculty Development Institute sponsored by the Professional and Organizational Development Network in Higher Education. One message that echoed loudly from that multiday institute is this: nurture, recognize, and support the faculty at your institution. They are the experts in their fields and faculty appreciate sharing their knowledge with their colleagues. It was decided that moving forward, our faculty would be invited as peer consultants to speak alone or in conjunction with other faculty on myriad topics.

Box 8.11

Refocus workshops from external-sponsored program to internally produced events. Nurture, recognize, and support the faculty at your institution. They are the experts in their fields, and they appreciate sharing their knowledge with their colleagues.

At the annual fall semester convocation, faculty were asked to complete a second survey detailing programs they would like to see offered during the upcoming academic year. Ninety-three surveys were returned; we had a captive audience. Among the topics that generated the most interesting were assessing student learning, laptops and cell phones in the classroom, peer collaboration (talking about what we do as teacher-scholars), and *how to give students feedback.* Other topics also received numerous votes: academic integrity, assigning and responding to students' writing, teaching and mentoring international students, finding a work–life balance, and service learning. Other write-in ideas were offered by the faculty.

The initial program focused on formative assessment. More than 30 faculty attended to hear from five colleagues about assessment tools in the classroom. The value of Google Forms and Question Pro were discussed and faculty were advised to consider giving students a note card to detail a lecture or homework assignment. A follow-up Google Forms and Question Pro program was held later at faculty request.

Next, the use and potential misuse of cell phones, tablets, and personal devices took center stage. Almost two-dozen faculty discussed the challenges and opportunities of mobile technology including allowing students to use these devices for specific in-class assignments. Shortly thereafter, the

CITADEL director met with the coordinator of the university's Black Male Leadership Development Institute about its own student-focused program. *Smartphone: My Enemy and My Friend* brought together 30 students to examine how these ubiquitous phones can distract from the professional and learning environments.

The Innovative Teaching coordinator also offered weekly *Teaching Tips* e-mail during the semester. Her messages highlighted academic research pertaining to teaching or technology, assessment, cheating, and other topics. These messages were delivered in a "you might find this important" style that required neither a reply from the faculty nor mandatory implementation in the classroom. As with so many items that are found on the Internet, *Teaching Tips* were designed to generate conversations and sharing.

Box 8.12

Teaching Tips make for an excellent communication tool between center leaders and faculty. Be sure to offer both pedagogical and technological pointers.

During Year 3 we launched a New Faculty Community. Eleven newly hired faculty joined RMU at the beginning of the academic year. Some were new to higher education. Others were new to the local community. Still others were embarking on their first full-time academic position. Beginning in September, monthly events were planned just for them.

Box 8.13

Launch a New Faculty Community for newly hired faculty. Beginning in September, monthly events were planned throughout the year just for them.

At the first meeting, the university's director of institutional research spoke about a favorable report that found our graduates more engaged in the workplace when compared to the national average. The IRM was introduced as our model for integrating pedagogy and technology in the classroom.

Two programs promoted faculty interactions with other faculty. Four recipients of the university's Distinguished Teaching, Research, and Service Awards spoke to the new faculty about building and sustaining a record in those three areas. Along with their colleagues, new faculty addressed "What I Wish I Knew during My First Year at RMU." These sessions did not include formal presentations; rather, a single leading question started a conversation that faculty took over from there.

Later in the academic year, a new program, "Teachers Noticing Teachers," was launched by the CITADEL. Faculty invited colleagues to attend a class and uncover how he or she applies the craft of teaching. A nominating process called for four faculty to self-select to showcase their personal brand of teaching. Two faculty welcomed colleagues during the first seven weeks of the semester, and the other two during the second half of the term. It is important to note that the program was not intended to evaluate how host instructors taught their class. Rather, it was an opportunity to see new ideas or strategies in action that might work in other courses.

Box 8.14

"Teachers Noticing Teachers" offers faculty an opportunity to invite colleagues to attend their class and uncover how he or she applies the craft of teaching.

8.6. LESSONS LEARNED

Do not get caught up in titles. Overlapping terms such as *workshop*, *roundtable*, and *brown-bag* were unnecessary and perhaps confusing. The intention might have been good, but at the end of the day, faculty will attend your programs not for their label but for the information that is transmitted and its effective delivery.

Box 8.15

Pick a label for your program events and stick with it. Do not make the mistake of confusing your intended audience with terminology.

Do not make the mistake of assuming that administrators are not interested in your center's activities. They will ultimately determine the success or failure of your center. Alert them in advance of workshops, surveys, and PLNs. Acknowledge contributions from their faculty with direct letters of appreciation. Ask them for input and advice. Department heads and deans have a much better understanding of what their faculty are doing as teachers and researchers. They also have a wealth of institutional knowledge about their school specifically and the university as a whole. Ask how your center can become involved in activities and events taking place in their school – perhaps, these opportunities can be adapted to university-wide programs.

Box 8.16

Regular and meaningful communication with department heads, deans, and upper-level administrators is a must. Ask them for input and advice.

Consider a strategic plan as a necessary first step in the maturation of your Center for Teaching Excellence. Two important factors aided the director in writing their strategic plan. First, the university had recently revised its own five-year strategic plan. The alignment of the CITADEL's strategies and goals could be enmeshed within the larger university plan and become operational quickly and for the next five years. Second, the academic units also were completing their plans; thus, there was an opportune moment to examine what these units were doing and to incorporate some of their ideas into the CITADEL's strategic plan. In short, the creation of the CITADEL, timed as it was with the new university strategic plan, allowed for a more streamlined process in completing its strategic plan. It took five drafts to get the plan ready for examination and approval by the senior administration. But it was worth it.

The key elements of a strategic plan are found at Appendix I.

Box 8.17

Align your center's strategies and goals with the larger university mission, vision, and plan.

8.7. CONCLUSIONS

There is no one best way to start a center of excellence. Among the issues that you need to consider when launching such an initiative are as follows:

- Sharing the Culture of Your Institution. If the focus of your center of excellence is on teaching, a system for recognizing good teaching is at the top of the list. The notion, true or not, of *publish or perish* at a research-based institution will erode the perceived value of a teaching center on your campus. On the other hand, the intrinsic value of teaching inherent with being at a liberal arts or non-research intensive university should be an aid in growing the teaching skills of colleagues. Especially when coming from another institution, faculty must be acclimated to the culture of the campus before making important judgments about the perceived value of your center.

- Understanding the Historical Relationship between Administration and Faculty. Faculty feel empowered when they are comfortable that administration will support and reward them for their efforts. Only then will they step forward. If there is an atmosphere of distrust based on rumors, past conduct, or simple lack of communication, their willingness to form and sustain a center of excellence will diminish. One of the messages repeated loudly and clearly during the academic year was that faculty involvement was critical in everything the center would pursue. Whenever possible, the faculty must play a legitimate role in identifying important initiatives.
- Adopting Initiatives on Your Campus that Succeed. Whether creating a new center of excellence or adding to the successes of an existing center, ask a lot of questions. Keep the good and learn from failures or missteps. If your center is advertised as faculty-friendly, make sure faculty are at the heart of everything you do. The message is clear: you dictate and you lose.
- Tapping into Webinars Hosted by Outside, Reputable Agencies. Multiple occasions arose during the first three academic years for center-hosted workshops to be sponsored by outside organizations. Such opportunities should not become an exclusive feature of your center, but they make an excellent source of expert training during a start-up period as you build a team to deliver your own locally developed content.
- Working Closely with Your Technology Department. No matter how much you know about technology, the professionals in IT know more. They live it each day. They install, repair, and update technology. Use their knowledge to build your center's website. Rely upon them for technological solutions that make learning easier. Make them partners in the center for excellence.
- Hosting a Conference. Build into your center's strategic plan a goal to host conferences in the coming years to examine important issues pertaining to engaged learning, civic engagement, or service learning. These gatherings allow administrators, faculty, staff, and students to share best practices, network with colleagues, and present relevant new research. They also alert other schools that your institution is a leader in innovative teaching and learning.

The CITADEL's formative years on the RMU campus are offered as a case study for other institutions. We offer curriculum, venues, and lessons learned for your consideration. And, we all have more to learn from you. Please consider joining our *IRM-Higher Ed Network* (for more information, see chapter 10).

Chapter 9

Faculty Portfolios for Teaching Excellence

9.1. INTRODUCTION

Portfolios have been used for decades to validate learning and performance: by faculty to support their arguments for tenure and promotion and by students to validate academic progress toward their degree and evidence of achievements for a first job. Portfolios provide individualized formats for presentation, folders for images and video artifacts, room for certificates of completion, and ready access to interested and multiple reviewers. Portfolios are living documents ideally developed and revised over a life-long career.

Accrediting agencies embrace portfolios as a repository of evidence as they evaluate how well institutions are meeting the needs of faculty and students. Johnson, Hsieh, and Kidwai suggest that portfolios "position (users) as producers of knowledge instead of simply consumers of knowledge" (2007, p. 380). Students feel this sense of empowerment as they transition from university to their vocation, and faculty as they move up the ladder of a professional career in higher education. Research has also shown a correlation between sustained portfolio use and higher grade point averages (Eynon, Gambino & Torok, 2014).

Portfolios often take the form of (sometimes several) three-ring binders or pocket accordion files. Hard copy portfolios are not dependent on technology (i.e., laptop or desktop computers) to showcase their contents, but they can be bulky and cumbersome when accompanying a candidate on an interview – not to mention intimidating to an interviewer with little time to peruse a hefty document.

Twenty-first-century technology offers e-portfolios as a repository for evidence of professional development. They can be created internally by an institution to serve its specific interests and needs, adopted from an open source application, or developed using commercial off-the-shelf software tools. For a substantive review and analysis of these options, the reader is encouraged to see *An Overview of E-Portfolios* (Lorenzo & Ittelson, 2005).

Beck, Livne, and Bear (2005) offer an important caveat when designing portfolios. They suggest that portfolios should incorporate formative strategies, including personal reflections and avoid summative strategies. The authors contend that summative e-portfolios did not "contribute to teacher professional development as strongly as did other portfolios" (p. 234).

We will make no recommendation as to hard copy or e-portfolio here. For faculty pursuing professional development, either modality will serve to document professional growth. And, while there is no standard design for a portfolio, there are certain recommended components that must be considered when constructing a portfolio.

9.2. CONSTRUCTING A FACULTY PORTFOLIO

A suggested outline of sections to include in your portfolio and information appropriate for each section is shown in Figure 9.1. Be aware that you may collect more information in some sections than others. Some faculty have more direct teaching roles, while others have greater administrative duties. So, faculty portfolios should be designed to be flexible enough to emphasize certain areas and place less emphasis on others. Let's explain further.

9.2.1. Executive Summary and Table of Contents

Prepare an executive summary to be placed in the front of the portfolio. It can be as short as a single page but should not exceed five pages. It should provide the reviewer with a road map for what they will see throughout your portfolio. It should highlight key points that you want to emphasize about your progress as an educator and how the portfolio reflects that information.

9.2.2. Personal Information

Include name and contact information; current position held (academic rank); subject area/academic discipline; work history; and center activities attended.

9.2.3. Teaching Philosophy

This is a short, well-considered statement that addresses your personal approach to teaching and learning; theoretical underpinnings of your teaching

Faculty Portfolios for Teaching Excellence

CONTENTS OF AN EFFECTIVE FACULTY PORTFOLIO

9.2.1. Executive Summary

9.2.2. Personal Information

9.2.3. Teaching Philosophy

9.2.4. Teaching Activities
    9.2.4.1. Direct teaching
    9.2.4.2. Curriculum development
    9.2.4.3. Scholarship

9.2.5. Mentoring/ Service

9.2.6. Administration and Leadership

9.2.7. Professional Development
    9.2.7.1 IRM Apprentice Integrator Artifacts
    9.2.7.2 IRM Pedagogical Integrator Artifacts
    9.2.7.3. IRM Technological Integrator Artifacts
    9.2.7.4.IRM Journeyman Integrator Artifacts
    9.2.7.5. IRM Master Integrator Artifacts

9.2.8. Recognition, Honors, Awards

9.2.9. Long-term Goals

Figure 9.1 Constructing a Faculty Portfolio. *Source*: Author-developed for this book.

approach (e.g., pedagogy vs. technology); reflections of your teacher–learner interactions; educational goals; and your role as a faculty member.

9.2.4. Teaching Activities

This addresses three broad categories: direct teaching activities, curriculum development, and scholarship.

> *Direct teaching* conveys information about quantity of teaching and quality of teaching. Data can include student evaluations, peer evaluations, and letters evaluating teaching effectiveness. Documentation should be in as clear a manner as possible and may include tables, graphs, or figures to express the information.

Curriculum development describes innovative educational activities you created or implemented, such as courses, text and web-based materials, syllabi, and assessments.

Scholarship holds scholarly materials produced and published to document your experience and establish your expertise. Scholarship represents teaching improvements or innovations disseminated in some way for peer review and critique, curriculum, and educational research.

9.2.5. Faculty Service

Faculty service gathers evidence of opportunities including doctoral and other committee work. This distinguishes between satisfactory service that is expected of all faculty and service that represents a contribution of some significance. Service as faculty work recognizes contributions in at least one of these areas: teaching, research, and service. Service as part of a scholarly agenda reflects disciplinary expertise brought to bear on initiatives that serve the community, the profession, or the university.

9.2.6. Educational Administration and Leadership

Leadership positions include course director, program director, committee chairmanship, principal grant investigator, accreditation reviewer, and more. This category includes administrative responsibilities for academic teaching programs. The description of each activity can be presented in tabular or short narrative format and should include the following: concise description of the activity, duration and site of the activity, purpose of the initiative, financial resources secured to support the position, any accreditation citations, assessment tools, quality improvement initiatives related to the program, and other pertinent information.

9.2.7. Professional Development

This section should include evidence of participation in your center of teaching excellence at each of the five quadrants of the Integrated Readiness Matrix. Collect artifacts from workshops (e.g., syllabi/agendas, handouts, and certificates of completion). This is our favorite section!

9.2.8. Recognition, Honors, and Awards

This component of a portfolio recognizes that faculty is the core of the teaching and learning and distinguishes your institution as one that promotes excellence and student success. Most schools recognize faculty as teachers, scholars, and advisors.

9.2.9. Long-Term Goals

Reflect on your long-term goals as an educator, including educational interventions, plans to improve your skills as an educator, and publications of your work as an educator. Reflections might be the most powerful item of any portfolio because it is through that process of thinking about what was learned and then how it was applied in a real-world setting that professional identities are built, Reflection also connects learning across multiple courses, formulates abilities to assess according to a particular industry's standards, and suggests future areas of academic or professional growth.

9.3. EVALUATING FACULTY PORTFOLIO

The academic literature identifies areas of discomfort regarding e-portfolios. Haverkamp and Vogt (2015) state that "concerns related to the amount of time needed to create and maintain ... portfolios; frustration with the process if clear directions for use, assessment, and evaluation are not provided; security of the viewing audience; and perception of self-advertisement if meaningful reflection of content is absent" are among the potential shortcomings (p. 286).

Parker notes that the general perception that the portfolio is outwardly focused – meaning finding a professional position – clashes with university leaders' contention that it is inwardly focused – meaning determining a program's effectiveness (2012, p. 99). Strudler and Wetzel (2005) report that unless faculty have relevant buy-in to the selection and implementation of the portfolio, they could feel that the process is being forced upon them. Moreover, the authors note that deans must provide overt support by, among other things, ensuring that the staff is in place to assist in establishing and monitoring the portfolio development.

The quality and frequency of feedback might be the biggest stumbling block to a portfolio. Peacock, Murray, and Scott (2011) see value in feedback coming from peers, instructors, and supervisors; self-evaluation is also valued. Lorenzo and Ittelson (2005) offer important caveats for any person or institution that is adopting an e-portfolio (although most of their admonitions apply equally to traditional portfolios). They include concerns about hardware and software, internal technological support, security and privacy, ownership and intellectual property, assessment of the effectiveness of the portfolio, and acceptance and long-term maintenance.

Name _____

Concept	Unsatisfactory	Insufficient	Exemplary
Elements:	Less than 80% of the required elements	80-100% of the required elements	Includes 100% of the elements
Organization	Little or no evidence of the ability to organize material	Overall well organized	Well organized, easy to locate artifacts, follows professional growth of faculty
Quality	Makes a poor visual impact. Contains numerous distracting mechanical, visual or grammar errors.	Good visual impact. Few errors to distract from content.	Well-written and presented for ease of review
Artifacts (Teaching, Scholarship, Service)	Insufficient TSS artifacts to support argument for professional growth	Sufficient TSS artifacts to support argument for professional growth	Exceptional number of artifacts to support argument for professional growth
Long-term Goals	Long-term faculty goals are missing	General long-term goals are included in the portfolio	Specific goals are included in the portfolio

Figure 9.2 Faculty E-portfolio Evaluation Form. *Source*: Author-developed for this book.

9.4. CONCLUSIONS

Faculty should begin using a portfolio early in their academic career rather than waiting until a promotion and tenure deadline approaches. Your Center for Teaching Excellence can aid its faculty in this endeavor by providing a binder or jump drive at an appropriate workshop on portfolio development. Ideally, such a workshop will be offered at the beginning of every academic year and target all faculty, particularly those who are newly hired, approaching a promotion and tenure milestone, or are not regular attendees at center events.

REFERENCES

Beck, Robert J., Nava L. Livne, and Sharon L. Bear (2005). "Teachers' Self-Assessment of the Effects of Formative and Summative Electronic Portfolios on Professional Development." *European Journal of Teacher Education* 28(3), 221–244.

Eynon, Bret, Laura M. Gambino, and Judit Torok (2014). "What Difference Can ePortfolio Make? A Field Report from the Connect to Learning Project." *International Journal of ePortfolio* 4(1), 95–114.

Haverkamp, Jacqueline J. and Marjorie Vogt (2015). "Beyond Academic Evidence: Innovative Uses of Technology Within E-Portfolios in a Doctor of Nursing Practice Program." *Journal of Professional Nursing* 31(4), 284–289.

Johnson, Glenn, Pei-Hsuan Hsieh, and Khusro Kidwai (2007). "Perceived Value of Persistence of Web Publishing Skills: Implications for e-Portfolio Systems." *International Journal on E-Learning* 6(3), p. 379-394.

Lorenzo, George and John Ittelson (July 2005). "An Overview of E-Portfolios." *Educause Learning Initiative* white paper.

Miller, Ross and Wende Morgaine (2009). "The Benefits of E-Portfolios for Students and Faculty in Their Own Words." *Peer Review* 11(1).

Parker, Michele (2012). "Qualitative Analysis of Student Perceptions of E-Portfolios in a Teacher Education Program." *Journal of Digital Learning in Teacher Education* 28(3), 99–107.

Peacock, Susi, Sue Murray and Alison Scott (2011). "The Transformative Roles of ePortfolios: Feedback in Healthcare Learning." *International Journal of ePortfolio* 1(1), 33-48.

Strudler, Neal and Keith Wetzel (2005). "The Diffusion of Electronic Portfolios in Teacher Education: Issues of Initiation and Implementation." *Journal of Research on Technology in Education* 37(4), 411–433.

Chapter 10

Invitation to Join the IRM Network

10.1. INTRODUCTION

You are invited to join the *IRM Higher Ed Network*, an online forum to expand your personal professional development by networking with higher education faculty worldwide. Membership is free and brings together educators who are eager to share their best practices and experiences with peers and colleagues. As a member of *IRM Higher Ed Network*, you will become part of a collaborative personal learning network (PLN) of knowledgeable and experienced educators from around the globe.

IRM Higher Ed Network is hosted as a Facebook page. To request membership to the site, please log into your Facebook account and send a *Join request* to *IRM Higher Ed Network*.

The *IRM Higher Ed Network* offers the following:

- A no-cost community membership to continue your journey into the world of higher education teaching. The PLN will announce upcoming webinars, research, and global networking opportunities with learning experts via our social networks and community forums.
- Opportunities for research to help expand your pedagogical and technological knowledge to deliver the optimal education experience. The PLN focuses on specific research disciplines and encourages collaboration with colleagues who have similar research interests.
- A higher education News Page to deliver the latest international, national, and regional information pertaining to teaching and learning.
- A forum for expanding your skills and competencies leading to Master Integrator as described in this text. As pedagogy advances and technology matures, this forum will help you stay current in these two critical

domains by enhancing specific proficiencies based on the suggestions of our contributors.

In order to promote these goals, this chapter introduces the concept of a PLN in general and the *IRM Higher Ed Network* specifically and extends a formal invitation to our readers.

10.2. WHAT IS A PLN?

PLNs have their origin in connectivism theory (Siemens, G. & Downes, S., 2005). Chapter 1 of this text introduced connectivism as one of the five schools of educational psychology and one of the most contemporary theoretical frameworks for understanding learning. In connectivism, learning and knowledge are built by connecting to and gathering information from others in a shared community. Siemens (2004) states that A (learning) community is the clustering of similar areas of interest that allows for interaction, sharing, dialoguing, and thinking together."

In the connectivist model, learning communities are described as a series of interconnected nodes that are part of larger networks and the connection points that form these networks. They may be of varying size and differing strength depending on the information and individuals accessing any particular node at any given time (Downes, 2008). Knowledge is distributed across the network using a variety of formats – the World Wide Web certainly the most popular. Learning and knowledge are said to "rest in diversity of opinions" (Siemens, 2008, para. 8), including both the cognitive and the affective domains, thus impacting the learning process in important ways.

A PLN is all about making connections and building personal relationships. In higher education, for example, faculty, administrators, staff, and students are often separated by distance, time, and discipline. More often, college and university faculty view themselves as disparate rather than homogeneous. Regardless of geography, chronology, or pedagogy, PLNs answer questions, offer forums for sharing expertise, or provide venues for sharing best practices in the classroom.

A PLN is all about ideas and resources, collaboration, teaching, and learning. Philosophies, tools, media, skills, and competencies are available 24/7.

A PLN is a global learning network enabling people to access and share diverse perspectives on teaching, educational issues, and technologies.

There are multiple ways to create a PLN. We have opted to host our PLN on a Community Page of arguably the most popular social networking site: Facebook. The intention of this site is to offer specific ways that educators can use PLNs for the following:

- locating resources for the classroom, such as free websites and software;
- sharing lesson-plan ideas from master teachers;
- learning about new technology and how to integrate it into your teaching;
- seeking collaborative solution;
- finding interesting links to education news; and
- learning from fellow content-area specialists.

10.3. USING THE IRM HIGHER ED NETWORK PLN

Cultivating a PLN takes effort – considerable effort. It requires a commitment of time and energy; but the rewards can be significant. Not only does interacting within a virtual community satisfy the need for social interaction and connection, it can also provide a media for professional development, personal satisfaction, relevance, adaptability, and most importantly it may positively impact teaching and learning in higher education.

There are seven elements in our model (Figure 10.1) for a successful PLN. We will discuss how the *IRM Higher Ed Network PLN* intends to utilize each element to the mutual benefit of our online community.

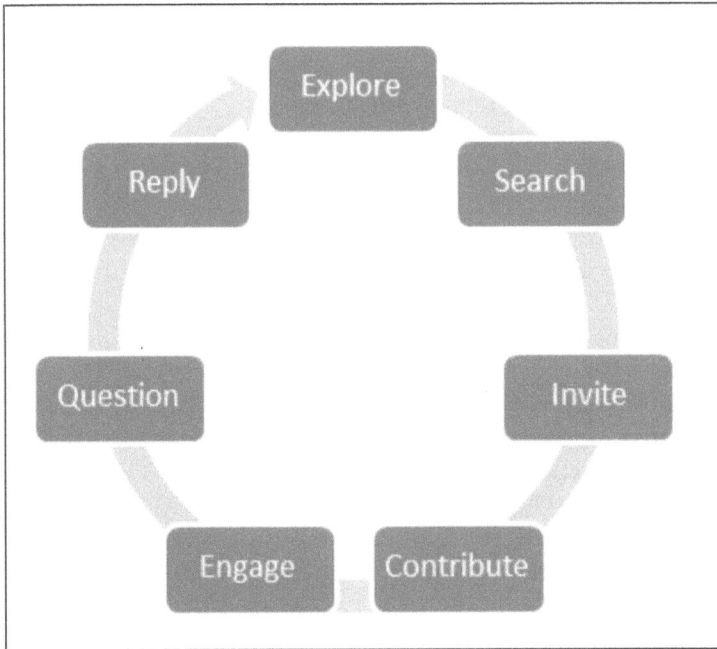

Figure 10.1 Model for a Successful Personal Learning Network. *Source*: Author-developed for this book.

1. *Explore.* This is a means of finding colleagues, content experts, and fellow learners; explore ideas and knowledge; expect to be surprised when your meanderings result in new ideas and take you in new directions; be open to new people, opportunities, possibilities, and knowledge.
2. *Search.* This helps to find nodes of expertise in specific disciplines of interest. As our PLN matures, we will be offering tools that will make the best use of our time online – tools that will capture web pages (or portions of them), assist in sharing ideas, or for finding relevant content. The goal of our PLN will be to add nodes of information focused specifically on higher education that will ultimately expand our own personal network and make us better faculty.
3. *Invite.* You can invite colleagues to the *IRM Higher Ed Network PLN*. Once you become familiar with the PLN, discover its nodes, and integrate its tools into your own professional development, you will want to share the network with colleagues and friends. Every individual who signs up for our PLN is another node with additional knowledge, different perspectives, and new opportunities.
4. *Contribute.* This step is critical to building the PLN. Nothing is worse than a PLN with *stale* information. *IRM Higher Ed Network PLN* will not be a monitored site; there will be no limitations to the contributions made by its members. A sure-fire way for any network to become obsolete is to depend on one or two members for new material. We will encourage contributions by asking members to visit the site on a periodic basis, post regularly, and take the initiative to share ideas.
5. *Engage.* You can engage with other members of the PLN; be conscious of other member's time when sharing; be courteous of their efforts; offer appreciation for new ideas and insights; ask questions; organize a discussion group; arrange a question and answer session; move the members toward a specific educational goal; post current events or best classroom practices.
6. *Question* You can question members about the status of their own professional development. For example, where are they on the Integrated Readiness Matrix? What is their institution doing to move them toward becoming a master integrator? What new skills and competencies can be added to those offered in previous chapters?
7. *Reply.* You can reply to inquiries made to you. An excellent technique for any online group is to *snowball* a discussion by posting a comment or idea, requesting replies from members, then replying back to their comments.

Finally, general *netiquette* rules of order suggest that all members become the kind of person that we all hope to encounter in any online discussion; set a good example; work to influence others, and they will respond in kind. Keep in mind that any electronic interaction is missing the nonverbal essentials of successful communication. The other person does not have the luxury of verbal cues from eye contact or facial expressions. The same rules pertaining to writing clear and concise e-mails and participating in online discussion groups apply to our *IRM Higher Ed Network PLN*.

10.4. ARE PLNS EFFECTIVE IN HIGHER EDUCATION?

If education is to move toward a more student-centric model as it appears to be (Downes, 2014; Drexler W., 2010), faculty have little choice but to model the shift from traditional, face-to-face instruction to more self-directed learning. If we are to inspire students to take more responsibility for their own learning, we must lead the way. We must show our support for lifelong learning by participating in the workshops and seminars offered by our respective institutional Centers for Teaching Excellence. We must evidence a commitment to lifelong learning by creating and participating in PLNs of our own design that may lead others to learning environments and networks of their own.

To encourage new members, we provide a handful of testimonials from experts already in the network. When you join the *IRM Higher Ed Network PLN*, you will be a colleague of these higher education professionals.

> I have learned that our PLN is a place for me to broaden my professional development as an educator. It is also a way for me to share resources that I have used and to offer advice and comments to other people. I use it whenever it is convenient for me to do so. If I want to work at 5 in the morning or midnight it doesn't matter. This is exciting!"
>
> The IRM Higher Ed PLN is a way for me as a new college faculty member to connect with other educators and not feel isolated no matter where they work or live.
>
> The PLN is well-organized, offering faculty a virtual room in which we can interact with other like-minded teachers. It allows us to collect information and resources from various sites to stay up to date on the latest teaching techniques, pedagogies, and tools for teaching. I also use it for social networking – maybe a new position at another university in the future.
>
> To me a PLN is an opportunity to learn whatever you wish to learn from people that are considered experts in that field – the IRM PLN is gathering those experts online. I strongly encourage your readers to become active – active! – members of this newest network for higher education faculty.
>
> It offers any individual with access to the internet a network of people willing to share information on a variety of subjects. With PLNs learning is accomplished on your own time, and how you wish to do it.

Figure 10.2 The IRM Higher Ed Network Personal Learning Network. *Source*: Author-developed for this book.

Professional development and personal learning networks – indisputable partners in growing higher education. Expert articles, videos, best practices – they are all there for the taking.

10.5. CONCLUSIONS

Our hope is that our invitation to become members of the *IRM Higher Ed Network PLN* will expand the network of higher education faculty and increase the number of Master Integrators of both pedagogy and technology. Join your colleagues on Facebook today.

REFERENCES

Downes, S. (2008). Places to go: Connectivism and connective knowledge. *Innovate: Journal of Online Education* 5(1). Retrieved January 2016 from http://nsuworks.nova.edu/cgi/viewcontent.cgi?article=1037&context=innovate

Downes, S. (2014). Personal Learning in a Connected World: Learning and Performance Support Systems.

Drexler W., (2010). The networked student model for construction of personal learning environments: Balancing teacher control and student autonomy, Australasian Journal of Educational Technology, 26(3), p 369–385.

Siemens, G. (2005). Connectivism: A learning theory for the digital age. Retrieved December 2015 from http://www.elearnspace.org/Articles/connectivism.htm

Siemens, G. & Downes, S. (2005). Connectivism: A learning theory for the digital age. *International Journal of Instructional Technology and Distance Learning, 2(1)*.

Appendix A

Dominant School of Educational Psychology

Do you agree or disagree that:	Agree	Disagree
1. Learners need grades, gold stars, and other incentives as motivation to learn and to achieve school requirements		
2. Learners should be graded according to consistent standards of achievement which the instructor sets for the class		
3. Curriculum should be organized along content paths that are carefully sequenced		
Do you agree or disagree that:	**Agree**	**Disagree**
4. Teachers need to determine what students are thinking about when solving math problems		
5. The teacher should help students monitor and control their own learning behavior		
6. Learning consists of building blocks of information that allows the student to effectively and efficiently adapt knowledge to new and interesting situations		
7. A learner's skill set is made up of several competencies including auditory processing, visual processing, short and long term memory, comprehension, logic and reasoning, and attention skills		
Do you agree or disagree that:	**Agree**	**Disagree**
8. Educational decisions should be made by the learner, personalized to meet their own academic goals and career ambitions		
9. The school experience should help students develop positive relations with their peers		
10. Students should set their own individual standards and evaluate their own work		

Appendix A

Do you agree or disagree that:	Agree	Disagree
11. Learners should have some options or choices in what they learn at school		
12. Faculty should develop a learning climate that is challenging, understanding, supportive, exciting, and free from threat.		

Do you agree or disagree that:	Agree	Disagree
13. For learning to occur, the learner must be actively engaged; that learning is not the passive acceptance of knowledge		
14. Learning consists both of constructing meaning and constructing systems of meaning; in other words, the task of the teacher is to help learners understand how they learn		
15. The critical component of constructing meaning is mental. Physical actions and hands-on experiences, while necessary for learning, are not sufficient		
16. Learning is not the accumulation of isolated facts and theories separate from the rest of our lives. We learn in relationship to what else we know and believe		
17. Motivation is essential for learning.		
Do you agree or disagree that:	**Agree**	**Disagree**
18. Knowledge originates and resides inside a learning community, a social network, or an information database		
19. Learning is a process of connecting as many sources of information as possible; a learner can improve their learning by joining as many networks as possible		
20. Nurturing and maintaining a collaborative environment is needed to facilitate learning		
21. Learning happens in many different ways. Courses, email, communities, conversations, web searches, email lists, reading blogs, etc. are the primary conduits for learning.		
22. Learning and knowledge rest in diversity of opinions		

Appendix A *(Continued)*

Appendix B

Action Verbs for the Cognitive Domain

Appendix B

1. Remembering	2. Understanding	3. Applying
Arrange	Annotate	Adopt
Define	Construe	Compute
Label	Convert	Develop
List	Defend	Exercise
Match	Discriminate	Manipulate
Name	Distinguish	Modify
Omit	Estimate	Produce
Outline	Extrapolate	Relate
Recall	Restate	Solve
Recite	Transform	Utilize
4. Analyzing	*5. Evaluating*	*6. Creating*
Assay	Appraise	Combine
Audit	Award	Compose
Break down	Censure	Design
Differentiate	Conclude	Develop
Dissect	Criticize	Dramatize
Distinguish	Decide	Formulate
Divide	Defend	Imagine
Infer	Grade	Invent
Simplify	Justify	Reflect
Subdivide	Validate	Rewrite

Appendix C

Action Verbs for the Technology Domain

Appropriate action verbs are underlined once, while the specific instructional technology introduced is underlined twice.

Action Statements for Technology Literacy

Access online data (budgets, databases, information literacy)	Label basic computer technologies
Capture digital pictures	Launch software applications
Cut, copy and paste text and images	Modify text color, size, font, etc.
Copy, move, and delete files	Navigate educational software
Demonstrate mastery of output devices	Open, save, close, drag files
Download text and images	Point and click to launch applications
Electronically transfer files	Select educational technologies
Employ search engines	Share files electronically
Format documents, presentations	Save/store selected files
Identify appropriate technologies	Scan images
Input data, URLs, etc.	Type, edit, print documents

Action Statements for Technology Collaboration

Communicate information digitally	Participate in a chat session
Create a desktop-published newsletter	Post current events in a newsgroup
Develop, edit, and submit digital reflections	Post messages to a bulletin board
Edit, revised, and resubmit a word-processed paper	Share information electronically
	Subscribe to an appropriate list-server
Email communications with parents/families	Survey comments via the web
	Upload senior class project assignments to the school's web site
Email fellow students	
Forward new links containing academic content	Work together via chat rooms in student groups
Investigate online web sites	
Interact electronically with other students	

Appendix C

Action Statements for Technology Collaboration

Analyze interactive help prompts and error messages	Develop a computer-based decision support systems
Assess data via statistical analysis software	Establish an historical student tracking system
Choose software menu and tools options	Interpret charts/graphs
Debate and evaluate alternatives for new technologies	Isolate, diagnose, and trouble-shoot hardware problems
Decide using spreadsheet analyses	Report using database capabilities
Defend computers in a laboratory environment	Track student achievement via grade book software
Defend computers in the classroom environment	

Action Statements for Technology for Learning

Add links to classroom websites	Download text citations and images Explore selected web-based sites
Assess the impact on student learning (evaluation) of infused classroom technologies	Harvest (select, download, and print) digital content
Capture textual content, visual images, auditory sound bytes, and video clips	Harvest sound bytes and video clips to support instruction
Conduct digital research	Prepare classroom web pages
Construct the visual elements of a technology action plan	Subscribe to electronic media
	Use internet multimedia search engines
Cut/copy/paste into a multi-page text-based document	Use web-design and editing software

Action Statements for Technology Integration

Broadcast a program on the school's closed circuit television station	Harvest from web sites
	Incorporate multimedia elements into a power point presentation
Build new enrichment materials in the curriculum inventory	Master text-based, visual-based, and web-based design technologies
Create an electronic progress report for parents	Prepare a visual representation to install and test CDROM software
Create a slide presentation that assesses the speed at which student respond to various stimuli	Produce a "front door" to a web-based virtual tour
	Produce a Hyperbook
Compose a helpful web-based form to assist parent teacher conferences	Produce an interactive lesson
Construct an electronic portfolio	Record a five minute video
Design a digital pamphlet for public relations for an imaginary business	Prototype a customized application using programming languages
Design workshop resources to include text-based online reports and publications	Use chart maker features to graph sales visually for an annual report.
Develop a boilerplate spreadsheet to capture daily sales figures.	

Appendix C *(Continued)*

Action Statements for Tech-ology

Use appropriate technology tools to determine the impact on student achievement of your school's technology program.	Become familiar with human factors that affect the use of technology for teaching and learning.
Consider using electronic mail, telephone interviews, video observations, and student record databases to gather demographic information.	Explore the evolution of technological advances from the perspective of contributions by a diverse group of people.
	Develop strategies for addressing a variety of access inequities issues.
Use appropriate technology tools to determine the impact on student achievement.	Consider the value of technologies for all students, especially those considered at risk.

Appendix C *(Continued)*

Appendix D

Recommended Teaching Episodes for IRM Quadrants

A.1 The Pillars of Education (Tomei, 2005)

Description: Philosophy, Psychology, Sociology, History, and Leadership are the pillars of teaching and learning. *Learning Outcomes*: The pillars answer several key questions on the design, development, and implementation of successful instructional strategies and learning styles; specifically: Philosophy answers the question "What are we teaching?"; Psychology addresses "How do we teach?"; Sociology involves the "Who are we teaching?"; History encompasses the "When (in the history of education) are we teaching?"; and Leadership focuses on "Whom [sic] are the key advocates of education?"

A.2 Learning Theories – A Primer Exercise

Description: The primary responsibility of teachers is to ensure student learning. A teacher's selection of educational goals, instructional strategies, and classroom organization and behavior is based in part on your beliefs about learning. **Learning Outcomes:** Teaching and learning strategies associated with the five major schools of educational psychology: behaviorism, cognitivism, humanism, constructivism, and connectivism.

A.3 First-Year College Students' Demographics

Description: Understanding the demographics of today's college freshman is critical to successful teaching in the higher education classroom. **Learning Outcomes:** A review of student demographics, student attitudes toward academics, first-year student behaviors, first-year studies programs, American freshman, and national norms.

A.4 College Student Subpopulations

Description: Understanding college generations and how college students have changed over the years. **Learning Outcomes:** A review of student subpopulations identified as traditional students, nontraditional students, online students; predicting the future based on demographics; select subpopulations of interest; and conclusions.

A.5 Historical Perspectives of Higher Education

Description: A solid foundation for higher education faculty necessitates an examination of the historical periods of higher education. **Learning Outcomes:** Review the recognized periods of higher education in the United States to include: the colonial period 1600–1776; the national period 1776–1865; university model 1870–1910; the golden age 1945–1970; era of adjustment and accountability 1970–1990; and twenty-first century 1990–2001.

A.6 Model for Differentiating Teaching and Learning

Description: The KARPE model offers the necessary distinction among educational programs in higher education. Mastery and competency at all previous levels are assumed at each higher level of the model. **Learning Outcomes:** Examines higher education from undergraduate, graduate, and doctoral perspective focusing on KARPE as the necessary distinction among educational programs in higher education. Assumed at each level of the model are mastery and competency at all previous levels.

A.7 Hierarchy of Human Needs

Description: Maslow's hierarchy should be compared and contrasted with other theories and theorists of human motivation. **Learning Outcomes:** Acquire a knowledge of Maslow's hierarchy of human needs and apply the different levels of physiological, safety, love (belongingness) esteem, and self-actualization) to scenarios related to higher education. Evaluate Maslow's hierarchy in relation to the US education system.

A.8 Taxonomy for the Technology Domain

Description: The six levels of the taxonomy for the technology domain to be explored include: Literacy, collaboration, decision-making, technology for learning, technology for teaching, and tech-ology. **Learning Outcomes:** List and define the six levels of the taxonomy of technology and apply the six levels to two different audiences with two examples of each.

A.9 Classroom Diversity

Description: Understanding classroom diversity and its many forms along with the challenges associated with diversity and current research on the topic is essential to effective classroom instruction. **Learning Outcomes:** Recognize what diversity is, including its many forms; become familiar with the challenges associated with diversity; and examine the current research on diversity with colleagues.

A.10 Servant Leadership

Description: This episode will examine the seven pillars of servant leadership and an exploration of what this style of leadership brings to the organization. **Learning Outcomes:** Know and comprehend the seven pillars of servant leadership and explore in a collaborative workshop or seminar what leadership means in a higher education environment, both from a faculty and an administrative perspective.

A.11 Academic Problems and Mental Health Challenges

Description: This episode explores a deeper understanding of mental illness among college students and introduces common diagnoses, causes of mental illness, available treatments options, the role of the faculty member, and the process of referring students to the Mental Health office. **Learning Outcomes:** Understand the prevalence of mental illness among college students; learn about common diagnoses and causes of mental illness; know your role as a faculty member and your institution's referral process.

P.1 Constructivism

Description: Constructivism is a school of educational psychology based on the idea that the learner is actively engaged in their learning process and the teacher is a guide in their self-directed learning journey. **Learning Outcomes:** Basic constructs of constructivism to include: learning is student directed; cooperative learning and socialization are important aspects in the constructivists classroom; students learn using critical thinking; and students are actively engaged in their learning.

P.2 Connectivism

Description: Connectivist learners exploit the ties between information nodes, recognize patterns of knowledge, connect to the world of individual knowledge, and develop and extend their own personal networks.

Learning Outcomes: Integrate connectivism into your own personal instructional strategies by understanding that: learning and knowledge can rest in a diversity of opinion; learning is a process of connecting specialized nodes or information sources; learning can reside in nonhuman appliances (i.e., technology); and capacity to know is more critical than what is currently known.

P.3 Teaching Behaviorally

Description: This episode presents an overview of behaviorist theories in higher education along with a review of the 6 levels of Bloom's Revised Taxonomy and Mastery Learning. **Learning Outcomes:** Differentiate between classical conditioning, operant conditioning, and social learning theory; identify the six levels associated with Bloom's Revised Taxonomy and Mastery Learning; and identify at least three behavioral strategies used in higher education.

P.4 Classical and Operant Conditioning

Description: This episode offers an overview of behaviorist theories (specifically, classical and operant conditioning) and its implication in higher education. **Learning Outcomes:** Recognize the important theorists and characteristics of classical conditioning and operant conditioning.

P.5 Reinforcement Schedules

Description: This episode presents an overview of behaviorist theories (specifically, classical and operant conditioning) and its implications in higher education. **Learning Outcomes:** Apply the principle of reinforcement, reinforcement schedules, including positive and negative reinforcement, reinforcement versus punishment, strengthening behavior. Also, be able to recognize best practices of how reinforcement schedules increase learning.

P.6 Social Learning Theories

Description: Understanding social learning theory and its implication in higher education provides a solid foundation for teaching. **Learning Outcomes:** Recognize the concepts and theorists of social learning theory; explain the modeling process as it applies to social learning; and apply social learning theory in the higher education classroom.

P.7 Programmed Instruction

Description: This episode presents a basic working knowledge and definition of Programmed Instruction (PI) to higher education faculty. **Learning Outcomes:** Define PI, identify its history (founder), purpose, function, and potential classroom applications. Consider real-world examples demonstrating the pros and cons of PI in a subject matter outside of general knowledge content.

P.8 Behavioral Learning Objectives

Description: Successful teaching involves writing behavioral learning objectives at the various levels of Bloom's taxonomy. **Learning Outcomes:** Identify, articulate, and discuss the elements of a well-planned behavioral learning objective, including action verbs, content/skill, and criteria for assessment. Match action verbs with their appropriate level of higher order thinking skills.

P.9 Zone of Proximal Development

Description: The distance between the actual developmental levels is determined by independent problem-solving and the level of potential development as determined through problem-solving under adult guidance. **Learning Outcomes:** Define Zone of Proximal Development (ZPD) and connect the foundational theories that formulated this concept. Compare the ZPD to scaffolding and analyze different types of scaffolding strategies that enhance teaching and learning in higher education.

P.10 Stages of Cognitive Development

Description: Stages identified by Jean Piaget are instrumental in forming the theory of cognitive development. **Learning Outcomes:** Understand the development progress associated with each stage of cognitive development as defined by Piaget: sensorimotor stage, preoperational stage, concrete operational stage, and formal operational stage. Match various famous Piaget experiments associated with each stage and apply the stages of cognitive development to the higher education classroom.

P.11 Cooperative Learning Theories

Description: Cooperative learning is a successful teaching strategy in which small teams, each with students of different levels of ability, use a variety of learning activities to improve their understanding of a subject. **Learning Outcomes:** Take existing lessons, curricula, and courses and structure them cooperatively. Tailor cooperative learning lessons to unique instructional needs, circumstances, curricula, subject areas, and students. Diagnose the problems some students may have in working together and intervene to increase the effectiveness of the student learning groups.

P.12 Individual Constructivism

Description: Key characteristics of individual constructivism provide examples of how individual constructivism applies to instruction in higher education. **Learning Outcomes:** Define *individual constructivism* and apply its characteristics to the higher education classroom.

P.13 Social Constructivism

Description: Key characteristics of social constructivism provide examples of how social constructivism applies to instruction in higher education. **Learning Outcomes:** Define *social constructivism* and apply its characteristics to the higher education classroom.

P.14 Assessment of Teaching and Learning

Description: Understanding assessment examines why assessment has become more critically evaluated in both teaching and learning. **Learning Outcomes:** Understanding what assessment is, its purpose in the higher education classroom, and how to conduct effective formative and summative assessment. Examine why assessment has become more critically evaluated in both teaching and learning.

P.15 Diversity of Learning Strategies

Description: This episode discusses various teaching strategies shown by research to be effective in educating higher education learners. **Learning Outcomes:** Recognize the different kinds of learners found in the higher education classroom and evaluate how different learning styles presented by the instructor can affect learning of the college student.

T.1 Open Education Resources

Description: Teaching and learning materials are freely available online for everyone to use, whether you are an instructor, student, or self-learner.

Learning Outcomes: Define *open education* resources (OER) and identify characteristics of effective OER resources for the higher education classroom. Give examples of using OER resources in teaching various college disciplines.

T.2 Online Teaching and Learning (Multiple Sessions Recommended)

Description: This episode explores the many pedagogical and technological aspects of online learning, synchronous and asynchronous learning environments, and online course planning tools in higher education. **Learning Outcomes**: Recognize the roots of online learning. Learn how to implement synchronous and asynchronous learning environments in the higher education classroom. Recognize online course planning tools in higher education.

T.3 Impact of Online Teaching on Faculty Load

Description: This episode examine the teaching demands for an online versus tradition course leading to class size, course load, and ideal head count. **Learning Outcomes:** Determine the ideal class size for an online versus traditional course. Recognize the teaching demands for an online course and the demands of an online course on faculty loads. Determine the delivery of content, assessment, and advisement demands on the ideal head count for an online course.

T.4 Massive Open Online Courses

Description: This episode explores the basic characteristics that make learning using MOOCs effective, the various approaches to delivering a MOOC, and MOOC-specific grading options. **Learning Outcomes:** Understand the advantages and limitations of MOOCs and the best sources of MOOC courses and determine some of the basic characteristics that make for effective MOOCs.

T.5 Faculty Attitudes Toward Technology

Description: This episode examines general information concerning knowledge of and attitudes toward information technology, including hardware and software, computer classrooms and labs, the Internet, and other technology devices. **Learning Outcomes:** Explore a number of core issues underlying faculty participation/nonparticipation in technology-related instruction which pose implications for policy and practice relevant to technology use and skills, training and development, course designed and technical support, quality issues, and workload and compensation.

T.6 Relating Technology to Theories of Learning

Description: Participants learn how to apply theories of learning, teaching, and instructional design and their relationship to the use of technology to support learning. **Learning Outcomes:** World changes created by technology lead to discussions of current student population and the role technology continues to play in higher education.

T.7 Educational Software

Description: Participants explore a variety of computer software-related issues including practicing responsible, ethical and legal use of technology, information, and software resources; research and evaluating instructional software for the higher education classroom; and developing recommendations for purchasing instructional software to support and enhance the curriculum. **Learning Outcomes:** Choosing an educational application to integrate into a curriculum can be difficult. Barriers such as the availability of time to learn the software, lack of funding for purchasing software, lack of teacher understanding of the connection between the technology and the curriculum, lack of technical support, age appropriate software, and an inability to access and try available material continue to inhibit teachers from selecting such technology for the teaching and learning process.

T.8 Communications, Networks, and the Internet

Description: Faculty examine how networks provide students a wide range of computer-based information resources from electronic libraries, person-to-person exchanges (e-mail, social media, etc.), and educational and entertainment. **Learning Outcomes:** Twenty-first-century skills are critical thinking, communication, collaboration, and creativity. Develop different pedagogies and learning environments to teach students how to think critically, communicate with others, collaborate on projects and be creative.

T.9 Technology Standards for Teaching

Description: A review of the technology standards is provided by the ISTE in the areas of creativity and innovation, communications and collaboration, research and information fluency critical thinking, problem-solving and decision-making. Curriculum, instruction and assessment should focus on meeting standards. **Learning Outcomes:** Effective teachers model and apply standards for teaching with technology as they design, implement, and assess learning experiences to engage student and improve learning; enrich professional practice; and provide positive models for their students. Review technology standards provided by the ISTE.

T.10 Internet Exploration and Harvesting

Description: Faculty demonstrate a grasp of instructional design and combine these skills with the use of technology resources harvested from the Internet to produce text, visual, and web-based materials for teaching. **Learning Outcomes:** Using the Internet to locate and download, save, and insert text, visual, and media-based resources for the design of teacher-made curriculum and instructional materials for the higher education classroom.

J.1 Effective Professional Writing

Description: This episode offers faculty support in the writing and editing process so that the entire process goes smoothly. **Learning Outcomes:** Explore: understanding the audience; developing a literature review; providing adequate support; writing with the reader in mind; crafting a strong conclusion; and preparing the manuscript for submission.

J.2 Guide to a Successful Book Proposal

Description: Faculty review guidelines that will help them plan and write a scholarly manuscript by following the steps of the publishing process. **Learning Outcomes:** Planning and writing the successful textbook; permissions; photo research and copyrights; submitting your final manuscript; and final thoughts.

J.3 Discovery and Reception Learning

Description: Participants become familiar with Discovery and Reception Learning as a tool for cognitive learning. **Learning Outcomes:** Identify differences between discovery and reception learning theories; connect existing knowledge about learning to discovery and reception learning; and apply discovery and reception learning to the higher education classroom.

J.4 Information Processing Model

Description: This episode introduces the Information Processing Model as a paradigm for cognitive learning. **Learning Outcomes:** Understand the steps of the Information Processing Model; identify effective techniques for transferring information from short-term memory to long-term memory; understand chunking and mnemonics; discern modes of retrieving information from long-term memory; and apply the model to the higher education classroom.

J.5 Andragogy: The Study of Adult Learning Styles

Description: This episode introduces the basic characteristics of adult learning and successful methods for teaching adults and its implication to the use of technology in the adult classroom. **Learning Outcomes:** Become familiar with the concept of andragogy. Apply Malcolm Knowles' 5 Assumptions of Adult Learners and 4 Principles of Andragogy. Introduce several different learning techniques and recognize established teaching methods of andragogy. Apply the concept of andragogy to the higher education classroom.

J.6 Psychosocial Development

Description: Faculty examine the basic characteristics of adult psychosocial development and its effect on successfully teaching adults. **Learning Outcomes:** Identify the stages of psychosocial development and apply the work of Erik Erikson to the higher education classroom. Recognize the importance of understanding psychosocial development terms to the adult learning.

J.7 Ethics in the Classroom

Description: Faculty are introduced to the critical nature of ethical conduct in the classroom. Faculty must dedicate adequate time to establish and reinforce those beliefs in the classroom. **Learning Outcomes:** Recognize the important concepts of academic integrity, intellectual property, copyright infringements, and APA style. Apply these principles of integrity in the higher education classroom.

J.8 Instructional System Design Models

Description: The Instructional System Design (ISD) basic model is simple to understand and easy to use in almost any instructional design environment. Essentially, it is a series of steps leading to the production of a successful instruction in the classroom. **Learning Outcomes:** Understand that a design model gives structure and meaning to an instructional task, enabling the designer to negotiate the task with a semblance of conscious understanding. Models help visualize the problem, break it down into discrete, manageable units.

J.9 Introduction to Instructional System Design

Description: Most ISD approaches contain five major phases: analysis, design, development, implementation, and evaluation. The outputs of one phase are the inputs to the next. This episode reviews the phases and describes their purpose, relationships, and results. **Learning Outcomes:** Identify characteristics of the ADDIE, Kemp, and Backward Design Model and apply its structure to the development of traditional and online college courses.

J.10 Learning Transfer Model

Description: Participants apply the skills, knowledge, and attitudes that were learned in one situation to other learning situations to increase the speed of learning. **Learning Outcomes:** Explore the different categories of learning transfer activities and its impact on learner readiness and learning transfer in the college classroom.

J.11 The Teacher-Scholar Model (Multiple Sessions Recommended)

Description: The teacher-scholar model challenges faculty to undertake intellectual activity that stimulates teaching and learning, forming an integrated process where various forms of scholarship and service complement teaching. **Learning Outcomes:** Understand what it means to be a teacher-scholar and appreciate the value of a teacher-scholar to the institution. Explore a newer, more progressive model of teacher-scholar.

J.12 Assessing Technology and Evaluating Student Learning

Description: Faculty explore several popular strategies for assessing both learning and teaching, from its more traditional applications to instruments that can be hosted online and evaluate technology-rich instruction. **Learning Outcomes:** Compare and contrast some of the ways in which technology can assess student learning using technology to perform the actions and cognitive processes a tutor would employ to arrive at a grade, and using technology to aid the assessment process.

J.13 Integration of Technology-Rich Resources

Description: The potential for technology integration is examined as another way to meet learner needs. **Learning Outcomes:** Technology integration as an instructional tool can provide ways to meet varied learning styles, assist in routine teacher tasks, and promote learning initiatives.

J.14 Creating Text-Based Student Materials

Description: Participants demonstrate how to construct text-based documents involving features, commands, and practical examples for building basic handouts and study guides. They continue to examine advanced word processing features that make the interactive, digital hyper book possible. **Learning Outcomes:** An examination of the features, commands, and practical examples for building basic handouts and study guides. The construction of the Hyper Book Lesson with more advanced word processing features.

J.15 Creating Visual-Based Classroom Presentations

Description: Constructing visual-based presentations begins with a look at the features, commands, and practical examples for building a classroom presentation. Constructing the Interactive Lesson presents the advanced features that move the presentation from a classroom, teacher-focused slideshow to an interactive, student-controlled learning experience. **Learning Outcomes:** A look at the features, commands, and practical examples for building a classroom presentation. Constructing the Interactive Lesson presents the advanced features including templates, word art, text color, drawing tools, and, most importantly, slide transitions and action settings.

J.16 Creating Web-Based Classroom Presentations

Description: Participants demonstrate how to construct web-based lessons and develop the Virtual Tour. **Learning Outcomes:** Examine the features, commands, and practical examples for building a single web page using Internet Explorer and Microsoft Word. Use advanced features of both packages to move the lesson from a classroom, teacher-focused display to an online, student-controlled learning experience.

M.1 Interprofessional Learning

Description: Faculty explore a working definition of interprofessional learning and cite examples of how higher education and research have been utilized in interprofessional learning. **Learning Outcomes:** Define interprofessional learning and offer practical examples of how it can be used in the higher education classroom. Develop your own perspective on interprofessional learning and its merits in the college curriculum.

M.2 Multiple Intelligences

Description: This episode presents the impact of Howard Gardner's theory of Multiple Intelligences; identifies the traits and skills of each type of learner; and provides concrete examples of tools/strategies to teach each MI in higher education. **Learning Outcomes:** Students learn in ways that are identifiably distinctive. Examine Gardner's learning styles: Visual–spatial, Bodily–kinesthetic, Musical, Interpersonal, Intrapersonal, Linguistic, and Logical–mathematical and design instruction that encompasses these different styles.

M.3 Integrated Readiness Matrix

Description: The Integrated Readiness Matrix (IRM) is a tool to identify the current level of teacher skills and competencies along two critical dimensions: pedagogical and technological. Locating faculty on the X–Y dimensions of this matrix can serve as a powerful professional development strategy. **Learning Outcomes:** Learn the characteristics of the IRM as it relates to teaching and learning and reflect on the IRM as a tool for professional development. Locate yourself on the IRM using self-assessment and the IRM instruments.

M.4 Personal Learning Networks

Description: PLNs consist of nodes where learners make connections with the specific intent that some type of learning and personal development will occur. Based on the connectivism school of educational psychology. **Learning Outcomes:** Join a learning network and extend your own personal learning network online. Demonstrate your ability to search for a specific hashtag. Identify how learning networks can be used in a higher education lesson.

M.5 Differentiated Instruction

Description: Participants are presented with the approach to teaching that advocates active planning for and attention to student differences in classrooms, in the context of high-quality curricula; that is, tailoring instruction to meet individual needs. **Learning Outcomes:** Analyze different strategies that support differentiated instruction and identify relationships to teaching in higher education. Demonstrate an understanding of the four classroom elements of differentiated instruction. Demonstrate best practice for using differentiated instruction in the higher education classroom.

M.6 Flipped Learning

Description: Faculty explore Flipped Learning as a pedagogical approach for higher education. **Learning Outcomes:** Acquaint faculty with Flipped Learning and identify and explain the four pillars of Flipped Learning: flexible environment, learning cultures, intentional content, and professional educator. Emulate the behaviors of a flipped educator by demonstrating best practice for using Flipped Learning in the higher education classroom.

M.7 Blended Learning

Description: The blended learning method combines the best of face-to-face and online methods to offer a dynamic method to the twenty-first-century student. **Learning Outcomes:** Understand connectivism and its contributions to blended learning. Learn the Goals, Models (Rotation Model, Flex Model, ala Carte Model, Enriched Virtual Model), and practices of blended learning. Learn ways of combining synchronous and asynchronous learning models into a blended teaching and learning higher education environment.

M.8 The Technology Façade

Description: The Technology Façade is defined as the use of technology in a school without benefit of a necessary infrastructure to support its application as a viable instructional strategy. **Learning Outcomes:** Examine the Façade by distinguishing its three parts: use of technology, necessary infrastructure, and viable instructional strategy.

M.9 Impact of Education Technology on Student Achievement

Description: Faculty explore research on the effectiveness of education technology on student outcomes over the past 20 years and examine how the integration of technology into instruction has become a strong positive impact on student achievement. **Learning Outcomes:** Even with the uniqueness of each school, classroom situation, and higher education, research evidence across studies provides consistent findings that enhance understanding of the role of teaching and learning with technology.

M.10 Faculty Experiences with Instructional Technology

Description: This episode investigates the relationships between student uses of information technology and other forms of student engagement. **Learning Outcomes:** Explore the use of instructional technology by faculty and its impact on their instruction. Understand faculty perceptions regarding time, efficiency, and effectiveness, as well as how instructional technology may have affected interactions with and among students.

M.11 Constantly Changing Technology World

Description: Technology has always been changing and this change is speeding up and, with it, ever-changing curriculum. As educators move toward newer modalities of learning, it is imperative that today's technologies present new ways of meeting these challenges. **Learning Outcomes:** It can be difficult at times to stay up to date with information technology. Explore some of the top reasons to stay abreast of the latest technologies in higher education.

REFERENCE

Tomei, Lawrence A. (2005). The Pillars of Information Technology. In David Carbonara (Ed.), *Technology Literacy Applications in Learning Environments*. Idea Group Publishers, Inc.

Appendix E

Building Your Own Teaching Episodes Template

Use this template to create your own teaching episodes

A.1 Title of the Teaching Episode									
Description: Overall goals and objectives of the episode									
Learning Outcomes: Specific results of the episode to include activities									
	Pedagogy				Technology				
Skill/ Competency	P-C	P-SA	P-T		T-H	T-S	T-SA	T-L	T-T

A.1 Title of the Teaching Episode									
Description: Overall goals and objectives of the episode									
Learning Outcomes: Specific results of the episode to include activities									
	Pedagogy				Technology				
Skill/ Competency	P-C	P-SA	P-T		T-H	T-S	T-SA	T-L	T-T

A.1 Title of the Teaching Episode									
Description: Overall goals and objectives of the episode									
Learning Outcomes: Specific results of the episode to include activities									
	Pedagogy				Technology				
Skill/ Competency	P-C	P-SA	P-T		T-H	T-S	T-SA	T-L	T-T

Appendix E *(Continued)*

Appendix E

A.1 Title of the Teaching Episode									
Description: Overall goals and objectives of the episode									
Learning Outcomes: Specific results of the episode to include activities									
	Pedagogy				Technology				
Skill/ Competency	P-C	P-SA	P-T		T-H	T-S	T-SA	T-L	T-T

A.1 Title of the Teaching Episode									
Description: Overall goals and objectives of the episode									
Learning Outcomes: Specific results of the episode to include activities									
	Pedagogy				Technology				
Skill/ Competency	P-C	P-SA	P-T		T-H	T-S	T-SA	T-L	T-T

A.1 Title of the Teaching Episode									
Description: Overall goals and objectives of the episode									
Learning Outcomes: Specific results of the episode to include activities									
	Pedagogy				Technology				
Skill/ Competency	P-C	P-SA	P-T		T-H	T-S	T-SA	T-L	T-T

A.1 Title of the Teaching Episode									
Description: Overall goals and objectives of the episode									
Learning Outcomes: Specific results of the episode to include activities									
	Pedagogy				Technology				
Skill/ Competency	P-C	P-SA	P-T		T-H	T-S	T-SA	T-L	T-T

Appendix E *(Continued)*

Appendix F

Integrated Readiness Matrix Survey Instrument

Check which Objective most closely matches an objective in your own syllabi		✓	
Maximum Points Recommended for this response		PR	
Transcribe Points Awarded if you selected this response		PA	
PEDOGOGICAL Learning Objectives	✓	PR	PA
01a. Given a map of the United States, the student will be able to label at least 45 of the 50 states.		1	
01b. After completing the class activities for the day, the student will predict what may happen next by creating a timeline of events as discussed in class.		3	
02a. Students will be able to correctly name the major bones of the leg and list five most common causes of knee joint pain.		1	
02b. Students will be able to distinguish between two major theories of learning and human development.		3	
3a. Given a series of polygons, the student will correctly distinguish among polygons by regularity, concavity, and line symmetry.		2	
03b. Given the dimensions of a rectangle, students will solve for its area by using the following equation: $A = l * w$.		4	
04a. Students will prepare a treatment strategy based on life-threatening potential of multiple traumatic injuries.		3	
04b. Students will orally present a new patient's case in a logical manner and differentiate between effective and non-effective testing & management protocols.		5	
05a. After completing the lesson, the student will discriminate the differences and similarities between the two main characters from Romeo and Juliet.		4	
05b. Students will apply Smith's five criteria to criticize a theatrical play and will justify their remarks.		6	

Appendix F

Appendix F

06a. Students will evaluate staffing assignments based on input from staff and assess approaches and corrections based on outcomes.	5	
06b. Students will create their own set of guidelines to determine the vulnerability of a manufacturing plant to localized corrosion.	7	
07a. Students will list five criteria for the evaluation of a theatrical play and give a rationale for each.	1	
07b. Given a series of math problems, students will be asked to explain how to convert between fractions, decimals, and percentages.	3	
08a. After this unit, the student will distinguish among types of polygons using the language of geometry.	2	
08b. Students will be able to employ statistical methods in an area where a specific model is warranted.	4	
09a. Students will develop at least five guidelines for helping staff learn from each other.	3	
09b. Given the results of relevant tests for determining heart-related problems, students will outline a plan for treatment.	5	
10a. Students will differentiate among the passages that attack a political opponent personally, and those that attacked an opponent's political position.	4	
10b. After discussing Chapter 5 in the text book, students will record and compare facts about the sun, moon, and the planets of the solar system.		
11a. Students will compare and contrast the most effective treatments from an array of presented options and choose the most appropriate treatment for the cases presented.	5	
11b. In the lab, you will be given a solution to see what elements make up the solution. Your task is then to design a series of chemical operations to separate each element in the solution.	7	
12a. Students should be able to describe at least 4 ways that communication skills help create a positive work environment.	2	
12b. Students will demonstrate the principle of reinforcement in actual classroom interactions.	5	
13a. Students will paraphrase the meanings of the 4 basic principles of communication.	3	
13b. Candidates will identify specific performance concerns with your staff asking for possible solutions and decide together methods of measuring successful outcomes.	6	
14a. After completing the lesson, students will be able to solve a numerical expression using the standard order of operations of parentheses, division, multiplication, subtraction, and addition.	4	
14b. From two pieces of sculpture from different eras and artists, compare-contrast to determine which piece you prefer and write a 2-3 page report defending your selection.	7	
15a. After completing the lesson, the student will be able to diagram the development of American social values based on cooperative learning and individual research.	5	
15b. Candidates will devise a yearly plan with staff to accomplish learning needs, supervision plan and rewards using the techniques discussed in class.	8	

Appendix F *(Continued)*

16a. Candidates will label at least three unique ways to approach staff whose performance is below expectations.	2	
16b. Students will illustrate which statements are based on facts versus which are based on assumptions based on our class discussion.	7	
17a. Given the geological ages of rock formations, students will estimate the relative ages from youngest to oldest of those formations according to the geologic time scale.	3	
17b. At the conclusion of the course, students will produce and defend a persuasive essay which takes a stand for/against teaching of sex education in elementary school.	8	
18a. Students will offer a 3-5 minute demonstration of how learning empathetic communication can help leaders provide constructive communication.	4	
18b. Working in groups and considering the current economic policies of the US that we have been studying, formulate your goals for employment, price levels, and rate of real economic growth for the next three years.	9	
19a. Students will list all 7 steps involved in locating the epicenter of an earthquake.	2	
19b. Using straight value depreciation, science students will appraise the merits of two copper-nickel alloys for the design of a heat exchanger.	9	
20a. After completing the activities, students will use organized data to discriminate among periodic weather observations during the course of a year.	3	
20b. At the conclusion of the unit, the student will create a visual representation of the water cycle from rain through evaporation.	10	
21a. Students will articulate the characteristics of each type of corrosion testing studied and describe how they can yield accurate corrosion rates.	2	
21b. Given a matrix of raw data, students will redesign a new table to represent meaningful change in average temperature of a local city over a 10-year period.	11	
Total Pedagogical Points Awarded		
Check which Objective most closely matches an objective in your own syllabi		✓
Maximum Points Recommended for this response		PR
Transcribe Points Awarded if you selected this response		PA
TECHNOLOGICAL Learning Objectives	✓	PR	PA
01a. Students will be able to select, load, and play age-appropriate digital and video content from the school library.	1	
01b. School will provide students with a collaborative network for sharing ideas.	3	
02a. Students will demonstrate at least 15 of the twenty basic technology features of a graphics software package to enhance their presentation delivery skills.	1	
02b. Students will use technology to enhance their skills for working independently and in small or large groups.	3	
03a. Each student will team up with an electronic pen-pal in Spanish 101. Students will send conversational emails written in language appropriate for the classroom topic area under consideration. Students will also receive a minimum of five emails.	2	
03b. Students will use technology as a data gathering tool to improve learning in geography, history, and other social studies disciplines.	4	

Appendix F *(Continued)*

Item	Score
04a. Students will use technology to think critically and solve complex problems.	3
04b. Students will view a one-hour Discovery Channel TV show on global warming and write a one-page critique of its major points.	5
05a. Students will participate in technology-based projects and activities using an integrated cross-curricular approach.	4
05b. Students will design technology-enriched learning environments to address curriculum objectives.	6
06a. Teachers will create the core of an online course, including learning objectives, syllabus and course material for at least two complete weeks of instruction.	5
06b. Teachers will use technology resources to address the needs of special education populations, including bilingual and special needs.	7
07a. Students will demonstrate proper use and care of computers and other technology.	1
07b. Students will use a podcast recorder to interview a famous expert in the field of medicine geographically separated from your school.	3
08a. Students will have access to the Internet for communicating with peers from a distance via networks.	2
08b. The teacher will provide instructional databases to help students expand their research/information processing skills.	4
09a. Students will use an Excel worksheet to enter data, use formatting tools, create formulas and use functions, and create charts.	3
09b. Educators will be introduced to the necessary technologies to support their own professional development and lifelong learning.	5
10a. Students will use technology in fine arts curriculum to explore and access ideas, feelings, beliefs, and creative expression.	4
10b. Educators will access curriculum materials from a variety of sources including the Internet and weave them into their presentation of curriculum.	6
11a. Students will design, develop, prototype, and exhibit public relations literature/materials for an imaginary business for a simulated board of directors meetings.	5
11b. Students will learn and practice ethical use of technologies that will prepare them for the 21st century workplace.	7
12a. Students will be able to correctly match at least 10 hardware and software computer terminologies items with their correct definitions within 30 minutes.	2
12b. Students will choose the proper features of chart wizard within the spreadsheet software to create different types of charts and graphs from the financial data collected.	5
13a. Students will be exposed to the tools of the Internet to include electronic mail, gopher, list-server, newsgroups, file transfer protocol, chat rooms, and bulletin boards.	3
13b. Students will work cooperatively using email and a discussion board to retrieve information to solve academic-related problems.	6

Appendix F *(Continued)*

Integrated Readiness Matrix Survey Instrument 141

14a. Students will use simulation software to design, build, and test solutions to real-world problems.	4
14b. Videotape a fellow student using the new Apple iPad device to download an app pertaining to an academic content area.	7
15a. After identifying the key characteristics of the greatest battle, students will select, download, and harvest digital content that best represents new information via text, visual, and web-based materials.	5
15b. Students will be aware of the multicultural world enhanced through access and communication with students and people throughout the world.	8
16a. Students will gather information using at least 4 different multimedia sources.	2
16b. Students will critique a You-Tube video that shows a stereotype of a career of their choice and have them defend their critique with evidence posted to a LMS bulletin board.	7
17a. Teachers will communicate at least weekly with students using the discussion board, virtual classroom and e-mail.	3
17b. Teachers will create an interactive study lesson of approximately 45-50 minutes for use in case studies and experiential application.	8
18a. Contrasting weather data from last fall, winter, and spring, students will interpret the chart/graph data and its impact and their rationale as to an appropriate month to schedule school intramural games during the upcoming school year.	4
18b. Students will consider ethical issues and esthetic point of view of the creative artist by placing representative original pieces of art on the World Wide Web for public access.	9
19a. The library/media centers within our school will become the hub of information access, including print, electronic, and multimedia resources.	2
19b. Given a model for visual-based instructional materials, teachers will harvest digital text and multimedia elements (images, sound, or video clip files) to create an appropriate interactive lesson.	9
20a. Students will interact synchronously (via online chat rooms) and asynchronously (via electronic mail) to discuss the impact of technology on human resources, financial markets, and the environment.	3
20b. Students will stay abreast of emerging networking strategies, including Wi-Fi and 3g connectivity to help ensure a long-lived and robust infrastructure for classroom application.	10
21a. Students will utilize developmentally appropriate instructional technologies (including e-books, podcasts, and word processing) to improve their reading, writing, and communication skills.	2
21b. Students should be able to recite the rules and recall the appropriate behaviors for using technology in school computer facilities.	11
Total Technological Points Awarded	

Appendix F

Appendix G

Robert Morris University's Student Engagement Transcript Categories

Arts, Culture and Creativity. This category allows students to explore how the arts, culture, and the creative professions make lasting contributions to our understanding of the world. On- and off-campus opportunities allow students to either create something that is exhibited or examine what someone else has done and then write a reflection from that experience.

Transcultural/Global Experience. This category provides multiple opportunities to visit a foreign country either for a short two- to three-week stay or for an entire semester. Students also can meet the requirements for this category through programs offered by the university's Office of Multicultural Student Services or the Center for Global Engagement.

Undergraduate Research. Under the supervision of a member of the Robert Morris University (RMU) faculty, students can complete a scholarly research project that is worthy of presentation at RMU's Undergraduate Research Conference or similar event. Many students can meet this requirement by successfully completing the capstone or senior-level research course in their major.

Service. Giving of time and talent for the benefit of others is another meaningful way to become engaged at RMU. If students complete 30 total hours of service with nonprofit organizations, they not only meet the requirements of this category but also feel a deep satisfaction that comes from helping other people.

Leadership. To become a leader of tomorrow, students are encouraged to start being a leader today. At RMU, they can be the head of a student club or organization and direct how that group completes important initiatives associated with the mission of that group. Or, they can mentor other students through various on-campus opportunities.

Professional Experience. RMU wants its students to be confident about their career choice and prepared to enter it. Through internships, field experiences, student teaching, clinical and similar career-focused efforts, students build their professional resume, network with professionals in their field, and increase their self-esteem.

Special Recognition, Special Projects, and Participation (Seventh Category). This category formally recognizes students who have exceeded expectations inside and/or outside the classroom. If they participate in activities that merit Student Engagement Transcript credit but do not fit in the categories above, they would be recognized under this category.

Appendix H

CITADEL Workshops

1. *Enhancing Academic Rigor* (Pedagogical Integrator)
2. *Flipped Classroom Basics* (Pedagogical Integrator)
3. *NVivo Statistical Software Package* (Technological Integrator)
4. *Inside Higher Education Webinar* (Master Integrator)
5. *Academic Integrity: Meeting the Challenge in Traditional Classrooms* (Pedagogical Integrator)
6. *Academic Integrity: Meeting the Challenge in Online Classrooms* (Technological Integrator)
7. *E-Portfolios Webinar* (Master Integrator)
8. *Distinguished Teaching* (Master Integrator)
9. *Feedback* (Journeyman Integrator)
10. *Assessment* (Journeyman Integrator)
11. *App-reciation of the App* (Journeyman Integrator)

Appendix I

Strategic Plan (Key Elements)

CENTERS FOR TEACHING AND LEARNING

Strategic Plan

University Mission Statement
Center Mission Statement
Key Initiatives And Strategies
Priority

Initiative 1: Advance Academic Excellence

1.1.1. Strategy: Prepare and deliver workshops that enhance pedagogy and technology
1.1.2. Measures of Success: Host five sessions during the academic year
1.1.3. Costs: $1000 for stipends and materials
1.2.1. Strategy: Create and maintain Personal Learning Networks
1.2.2. Measures of Success: Host two new PLNs each academic year
1.2.3. Costs: Minimal

Initiative 2: Increase staff size and professional development opportunities for faculty

2.1.1. Strategy: Develop and approve an organizational structure for the center
2.1.2. Measures of Success: Receive approval for the center organizational chart and a separate budget for center operations
2.1.3. Costs: Minimal

2.2.1. Strategy: Develop a staffing plan complete with headcount and personnel budget
2.2.2. Measures of Success: Receive approval for staff and budget
2.2.3. Costs: Stipends: $_____ Salaries: $_____

www.ingramcontent.com/pod-product-compliance
Lightning Source LLC
Chambersburg PA
CBHW030114010526
44116CB00005B/240